JOB

Norman C. Habel

KNOX PREACHING GUIDES
John H. Hayes, Editor

John Knox Press
ATLANTA

Library of Congress Cataloging in Publication Data

Habel, Norman C.
  Job.

  (Knox preaching guides)
  Bibliography: p.
  1. Bible.   O.T. Job—Commentaries.   I. Title.
II.Series.
BS1415.3.H3   223′.107   80-82193
ISBN 0-8042-3216-4 (pbk.)   AACR2

© copyright John Knox Press 1981
10 9 8 7 6 5 4 3 2 1
Printed in the United States of America
John Knox Press
Atlanta, Georgia 30365

Contents

JOB

Introduction

Preaching From Job

Preaching from Job is like nurturing a cactus garden. One is liable to recoil from constant prickles and miss the blossoms in the night. Patient and cautious negotiation of the text, however, will yield strong messages that touch the faith and fears of contemporary listeners. The spines and spikes of Job reflect a real world with which we can identify, especially when brilliant blooms are rare.

The book of Job is composed of a complex series of poems set within the framework of an old folktale. The folktale is like a parable of ancient life, a foil for the struggles of the author presented in the poems. The folktale and the poem present divergent images of Job; in the one he is a patient sage, in the other an angry antagonist of God. Nor do the poems present a common front. The ideas of Job conflict with those of the three friends. The answer of God from the whirlwind overrides the arguments of all the disputants. The anonymous wisdom writer of Job 28 argues that no one can discover wisdom anyway. Job is a mosaic of diverse theological ideas, mythic motifs, literary genres, and colorful rhetoric. Honest preaching from Job demands an appreciation of these subtleties.

In his speeches Job touches the quick of human suffering and the passion of real life. Once we read beyond the delightful folktale of the first two chapters, we are confronted by ar-

ticulate curses and blatant denunciation of God's ways. Job
and his friends berate each other as fools. Elihu explodes in a
youthful tirade of traditional answers. The anguish, pas-
sions, and struggles of human life surface in the language of
despair. The rhetoric of anger and frustration colors the
message of Job. The following guidelines are suggested for
interpreting the polarities and rhetoric of this complex work
of art.

The Text in Context

To appreciate a cactus patch one must view the total garden, the way it has been landscaped with paths, rocks, and
patterns of cacti. The structure of Job demands that the
preacher take into account the three major features which
dominate the book—the folktale, the debate cycle, and the
closing responses. These appear in the following units of the
text.

The Folktale 1–2; 42:7–17

The Debate Cycle
    Opening Curse 3
    Cycle One 4–14
    Cycle Two 15–21
    Cycle Three 22–27

The Responses
    Wisdom Poem................................. 28
    Job's Summation 29–31
    Elihu's Speech 32–37
    Yahweh's Answer 38–41
    Job's Reply 40:3–5; 42:1–6

Each piece of this literary work is part of an intricate
whole. Whether we designate the totality a sustained wisdom
disputation within a narrative frame or a serious traditional
comedy with the folktale providing a happy ending to a tragic
life expressed through a chorus of arguments about the meaning of life, is a matter of debate. In either case, individual texts
of the book cannot be readily taken in isolation as gems of revelation fallen fully polished from heaven.

Sermons based on the friendly folktale of chapters 1–2

should take into account the harsh cries of the poems that follow. Job has two sides; to consider only his pretty side and ignore the other is to do an injustice to his complex character. The idealized image of the folktale should be balanced by the angry despairing man of the debate. The folktale does not stand by itself. It is the ideal against which the real of the poet's world is thrown into bold relief. It is the foil for the truth of human experience proclaimed by Job in the dispute.

In preparing a sermon on Job 1–2, therefore, it is wise to take into account at least a selection of pivotal units from the poem to provide a sense of Job's agony. My suggestion would be to read chapters 3, 7, 12 and 16. These passages will present a sketch of Job as the victim of God's inhuman attacks: Job the man of despair, Job the berater of God as a tyrant and spy, Job the man in search of a mediator, and Job the plaintiff without a court to hear his case.

The speeches of Job should also be studied in relation to those of the three friends and vice versa. The issues of the debate are neither simple nor unambiguous. As background to a sermon on one of Job's speeches I would suggest reading the comments offered on Eliphaz' speeches in chapters 4, 5 and 15. The concerns of Bildad and Zophar are treated in the comments on chapters 8 and 11.

The closing responses of the book presuppose, in turn, the gist of the debate which has preceded. Elihu's speech attempts to draw together all the arguments in defense of God (chaps. 32–37). Job's summation serves as an oath and final challenge to provoke God's advent in court (chaps. 29–31). Yahweh's speech from the whirlwind beggars description. It is a masterpiece of poetic expression which tackles the problems of Job at a totally different level than in the preceding debate. To appreciate that new level one needs to have explored the preceding struggles of Job and his friends. Job's final words in 42:1–6 are ambiguous; they reflect the complexity of the preceding argumentation and the overwhelming mystery of God's appearance. Yet this text remains a crux for the interpretation and appreciation of the book as a whole. Job's final words may not be unequivocal, but they offer a closing comment with which we can identify if we have followed Job sympathetically in his quest for meaning.

Counterpoint and Canon

Cacti refuse to be confused with other plant life. They force sharp distinctions and rather unsubtle polarities. Similarly, Job refuses to yield a single image of truth. A passage from one speech in Job finds its counterpoint in another. Points and counterpoints are typical of the great debate. Opposing views about God, suffering, human nature, wisdom, and prayer recur throughout the book. The interpreter must walk a careful path between an avenue of opposites. We cannot begin with the assumption that one side of the avenue represents truth and the other falsity. Do Job's friends only speak error? Hardly! Should we always emulate Job just because God commends him (42:7)? Many of Job's speeches are so vitriolic they seem blasphemous. Both sides of the avenue may be beautiful.

The first avenue of opposites consists of the ideal world of the folktale and the real world of the poem. This contrast was discussed briefly in the preceding section. An array of ideal portraits from the patriarchal world are juxtaposed with the harsh images of Job and his friends in debate. The patient Job is contrasted with the angry Job. The perfect friends of the story become unsympathetic wisdom teachers. Yahweh, the God who allows Satan to plague Job with evils, challenges Job to gird his loins and overpower evil. The author takes us on a journey from the world of the folktale, through a forest of agonizing debates, into a land of happy endings. The interplay between dream and reality, childhood innocence and mature knowledge, pious example and rebellious model, or the romantic and the tragic are not only part of Job's world, they are also part of our world. Preaching in Job allows us to walk between these worlds and affirm them both. To endorse one without exploring the other is to fall into the same trap as Job's friends.

A second avenue presents opposing motifs drawn from OT theology and Near Eastern mythology. God himself plays many diverse roles in the book. At one point he may be the Lord of wisdom ordering the world to conform to his principles of cosmic justice. At another, he is accused of deliberately fostering cosmic disorder and injustice. Job admits that loving kindness was God's apparent motive for creating human beings with artistic care. Yet he condemns God for demonic harassment of innocent humans as if they were worthless prey. God is creator, ruler, victor over chaos, lord of wisdom, righteous judge, and merciful redeemer in one series of texts. He is merciless warrior, enemy, lord of chaos, hunter of humans, unjust accuser, spy, and destroyer in another series of texts.

Numerous motifs from OT theology are expressed in comparable sets of opposites. Human beings are born totally corrupt according to Eliphaz (4:17–19). They have a potential for greatness, retorts Job, but God prevents this expression of his image in man (see comments on 7:11–21). Only the wicked suffer punishment at the hands of God claim the friends (4:7). The innocent are just as vulnerable asserts Job (chap. 16). Death is a gloomy world of darkness from which God redeems his faithful (5:17–20). Death is an inviting refuge, replies Job, where all human beings are equal, the world is at peace and the insidious surveillance of God cannot penetrate (3:11–19).

From among the many polarities and oppositions of the book, we have selected a catalogue of reasons for suffering explored within the book as a whole. The positions range from God being totally responsible (or perhaps irresponsible) to humans as being the sole cause. The preacher has a panorama of options. All are expressions of the way suffering has been understood by God's saints:

(a) Suffering is due to direct attacks by a God who enjoys hunting down humans as prey. God is a hunter of men; they were created with the secret purpose of being game for God (see comments on 6:4–13; 10:8–22).

(b) Suffering results from the way God rules the world; he creates and destroys, blesses and curses, hurts and heals. His pattern is quite arbitrary. His rain falls on the just and the unjust. The animals know quite well there is no moral logic to when and where catastrophes or suffering happen in the world. It is the same with all of nature, including human beings (see comments on chap. 12).

(c) Suffering is sent as a trial to test the faith of believers and vindicate them before the court of heaven. Such trials may even be provoked by unseen wagers among the members of the heavenly council, perhaps even God and Satan (see comments on 1:6–12).

(d) Suffering arises naturally. We are humans created

from the dust of the accursed ground and therefore corrupt. As children of corrupt Adam we are heirs to the ills of
earth (see comments on 4:17–19; 5:1–7).

(e) Suffering is a discipline sent by the Almighty to en-
courage repentance, build character, foster obedience, and
educate the believer in the ways of God. Through suffering
the faithful learn reliance on God's power (see comments
on 5:17–27; chap. 33).

(f) Suffering is a direct punishment from God for sins committed by individuals, their families or community. This
teaching is grounded in the doctrine of reward and retribution typical of Deuteronomy and serves as the basis for
many of the arguments developed by the friends. The doctrine is a reproach to Job (see comments on 4:3–9).

The exploration of these opposites does not end with the
inner antitheses of the book. Counterpoint extends across the
canon. Both OT and NT writers present alternative expressions of the truths found in Job. The NT, in particular, represents a new polar vantage point from which Job may be
interpreted. The hopes of Job find surprising fulfillments in
Jesus Christ. The quest of the Joban poet is pursued along new
lines by the NT authors.

Job as the innocent victim has been interpreted as a type of
Jesus Christ, the victim on the cross. Job, however, demands
public vindication of his integrity. Jesus Christ suffers vicariously. Job longs for a mediator who will espouse his righteous
cause and force God to appear in court and exonerate him.
Jesus, the mediator, identifies with the unrighteous and appears before God, the judge, on their behalf (see comments on
9:25–25; chap. 19). Job looks for vindication and restoration
in this life as the evidence of God's ultimate justice. In Jesus
Christ, the righteousness of God is finally vindicated in the
resurrection of the faithful.

There are many polarities between Job and the NT. One of
the most startling is the vision of death and the underworld.
In Job, humans are one with Adam. They are dust and will return to the dust from which they came; Mother Earth will
welcome them to endless rest in her womb. Job knows of no
resurrection from the grave or heavenly home reserved for
God's saints. The grave is a refuge, a land of oblivion where
humans can escape the agonies of life on earth. Paul offers a

radically different prospect in which the fate of humans in Adam is contrasted with the hope of believers in Christ, the second Adam (see comments on chap. 14).

In the commentary on each of the passages chosen the internal counterpoint of Job is usually noted. At appropriate points a number of polarities suggested by the NT are discussed. They offer a fresh answer to the eternal quest for the meaning of life, suffering, and death. If we are one in Adam we are also one with Job—and potentially one in Jesus Christ.

The Rhetoric of Reality

The following refrain from a recent popular song captures the point of the preceding discussion and leads us to reflect further on the language of Job. The refrain runs

> I've looked at life from both sides now,
> From win or lose and still somehow
> It's life's delusion I recall.
> I really don't know life at all.

It is a weakness of much preaching that life is portrayed from one side only—that of the obedient faithful Christian. The examples of mature Christian life paraded before us are men and women of great faith who have found the answers. Answers fall from the pulpit like rain; the Christian life is depicted as a rainbow filled with promises and answers. The favored path is the yellow brick road to heaven; if we follow the signposts, the answers given along the way, we will arrive safely and avoid the cacti of life.

There is no yellow brick road through Job. Taken as a totality the book of Job offers an arduous quest for understanding and meaning in a world of suffering, injustice, and futility. Job reaches a new level of consciousness at the end of the book, but he offers no tabloid answer for others to swallow. They too must follow his ordeal. The point of Job is the process involved in the struggle for understanding; the language of the book enables the reader to experience that process vicariously. The rhetoric of debate, agony, frustration, anger, sarcasm, and scorn are reflected at appropriate moments in the text. The inner fears and feelings of Job are exposed with strong words. The spokesmen of the book are

portrayed as people of the real world arguing about ultimate
matters in the heat of a human crisis.

Most of the speeches of Job and his three friends com-
mence with sarcastic comments, belittling remarks or *ad
hominem* assertions. They rarely advance the argument. They
belong, rather, to the rhetoric or wisdom disputes of the ancient world. Bildad accuses Job of being full of "hot air" (8:2).
Eliphaz claims that Job is a poor listener. Zophar calls Job a
glib babbling fool (11:2–3). Job's response is a sarcastic retort: "No doubt you are perfect men and absolute wisdom is
yours" (12:2). With the following round of speeches the rhetoric of rebuff continues.

There is no overt theology in these opening onslaughts.
They highlight the language framework, however, within
which any theology or preaching operates. Luther's apologet-
ics were replete with similar uncomplimentary remarks
about his theological and political opponents. The rhetoric ac-
centuates the role; the form reflects the function. The medium
changes, however, with the culture and the context. The approach of Job or Luther may prove awkward in many pulpits
today. We have moved from the oldstyle harangue to the
warm tone of conversation, from fire and brimstone to fireside
chats and reasoned argument. Or at least some preachers
have!

The crucial question posed by the language of Job is not
merely what mode of communication is appropriate for pro-
claiming the Gospel message today, but whether, in fact, the
poignancy of the text is lost by its reformulation in more comfortable terms. There is not one comfortable word in the imprecations of Job's opening soliloquy (chap. 3). If Job is to be
heard his language must live. The role of rhetoric is to accen-
tuate the polarity, not to soften it. Only then can the depths of
the crisis be exposed or the significance of opposing positions
be appreciated fully. Has the language of the pulpit become
lukewarm? Will Job continue to be a voice crying from the
ashheap?

The rhetoric of Job's speeches sometimes borders on
blasphemy. His opening soliloquy is a string of curses; his
summation includes a defiant oath (chap. 31). He accuses
God of being an insidious spy, an inhumane hunter, and a
demonic foe. Job's friends may deride him as a fool, but his

God knows better. He is a powerful antagonist whom Job labels with all the epithets of an ugly enemy. Among the wide range of emotions expressed, the rhetoric of Job's anger is perhaps the most formidable. Job not only pleads with God, he lambasts him, attacks him, abuses him, baits him, and finally challenges him with an oath. Job pulls no punches. He refuses to submit meekly to the will of a fickle deity. His reactions are violent, his language bold, honest, and pointed. The following represents a brief selection from Job's rhetoric:

> How long wilt thou not look away from me,
> nor let me swallow my spittle?
> If I sin what do I do to thee, thou watcher of men?
> Why hast thou made me thy mark?
> Why have I become a burden to thee? (7:19–20).

> He crushes me with a tempest,
> and multiplies my wounds without cause.
> He will not let me get my breath,
> but fills me with bitterness (9:17–18).
> Though I am innocent, my own mouth would condemn me;
> though I am blameless, he would prove me perverse (9:20).

> When disaster brings sudden death,
> he mocks at the calamity of the innocent (9:23).

> If I wash myself with snow,
> and cleanse my hands with lye,
> yet thou wilt plunge me into a pit,
> and my own clothes will abhor me (9:30–31).

Sermons on Job provide an opportunity for God's people to speak the language of a rebellious, angry saint and to express the emotions of frustrated faith instead of suppressing them. Job offers a model of honest confrontation with God. He has the courage to denounce and demand, to force the Almighty to face the reality of what his actions mean for helpless mortals. In Job, we find an ally in our search for human rights before the court of heaven, the right to be heard when we are at odds with God (see the comments on 3:1–12; 5:8–16; 16).

A Lenten Cycle of Sermons

Relatively few passages from the book of Job have been selected for inclusion in contemporary lectionaries for the
church year. The propers for the day are therefore not likely to
stimulate preaching from Job. The Office of the Dead, which
arose in the Middle Ages, originally included the following
passages from Job: 7:16– 21; 10:1– 7, 8– 12; 13:23– 28; 14:1– 6;
14:13– 16; 19:1– 3; 17:11– 15; 19:20– 27; 10:8– 22. These texts
are appropriate for memorial services even today.

The Lenten season provides an appropriate opportunity
for a series of sermons comparing the passion of Job and the
suffering of Christ. The following sequence could be followed
as outlined or adapted for mid-week services. The cycle enables the congregation to experience the major struggles of
the patriarch Job in the context of Christ's suffering. The series could be entitled Portraits of a Suffering Saint.

Ash Wednesday: Job 2:1– 10
Affirming the Ash-heap
Job is first portrayed as a patient saint, bereft of all pos-
sessions. He takes up his vigil and affirms the ashheap.
He submits to the evils permitted by God without complaint or bitterness. Taken in the context of the Joban
folktale and in tandem with 42:1– 6, the motifs of Ash
Wednesday are given a specific focus. To be among the
ashes is to be human, to suffer as God's creature (see
Matt 6:1– 18).

First Sunday in Lent: Job 3:20– 25
Screaming for a Reason Why
Job's attitude changes from patience to frustration. He
questions the purpose of existence itself. God has surrounded his life with sufferings and rendered it meaningless. Job almost succumbs to the temptation to curse God
and die. In Gethsemane, Jesus too struggles with the cruel
way of the cross stretching out before him. When the saint
loses a vision of destiny, suffering becomes meaningless
(see Matt 4:1– 11; 26:36– 36).

Second Sunday in Lent: Job 6:14– 30
Yearning for a Loyal Friend

Job, like Jesus, is ultimately deserted by his friends. Genuine friendship demands loyalty in spite of all obstacles and opposition. The friends betray Job just as Peter denies Jesus. Yet Jesus befriends the woman at the well and Job's companions once knew empathy (see comments on 2:11–13). Saints who suffer their agony alone understand friendship and sympathy. They know when the old hymns of comfort are painful (see comments on 5:8–16 and John 4:5–26; Matt 26:69–75).

Third Sunday in Lent: Job 7:11–21
Yelling Back in Anger
Job's reaction to unjust suffering moves from frustration to fury. He claims that God is treating him as a monster rather than a human. He is an animal to be hunted as prey rather than a being created in the image of God. His plight is as unjust as that of a man born blind; Job has committed no crime. He is humiliated for no apparent reason. The ultimate purpose of Jesus' humiliation is likewise hidden. The saint who finds God the enemy discovers integrity in anger (see John 9:13–34; 18:19–24).

Fourth Sunday in Lent: Job 16:15–22
Demanding Human Rights
What are the rights of the suffering saint before God? From the deep of despair the question is far from academic. Job claims his assault by the Almighty is tantamount to murder. He demands a court where his innocence can be vindicated, a moment when God will communicate instead of harass him. Job wants a heavenly witness to testify on his behalf (cf. 9:25–35). The saint stripped of all rights is rendered an outcast. Jesus affirms the right of return but repudiates a right to glory in his kingdom (see also comments on 40:6–14 and Matt 20:17–28; Luke 15:11–32).

Fifth Sunday in Lent: Job 12:13–22   *Yom Kippur*
Hailing the King of Chaos
Rarely do we find God's saints engaging in satire. Job hails God as if he were the Lord of chaos. He challenges the way God in his wisdom, or folly, rules the world. His government appears quite arbitrary and even the animals

know it (see comments on 12:1–12). Is there ever an excuse for the innocent to be victims? Does even one man
need to die for the people? "Hail King of the Jews," scof-
fed the bystanders. At Calvary God seemed impotent to
prevent injustice and to silence the scoffers. Even saints
like Job may vent their spleen in the face of cosmic injustice (see John 11:47–53; 27:32–44).

Sunday of the Passion (Palm Sunday): Job 38:1–3; 40:6–14.
Troubled by a Talking Whirlwind
The saint who takes on God is likely to face unseen dilem-
mas. When Yahweh answers Job from the whirlwind he
poses a new set of riddles. He challenges Job's identity
and prowess. "Who on earth is this man?" asks God. Is he
the heavenly First Man? (see comments on chap. 15). The
heroic saint provokes wonder from humans and whirlwinds from God. The question of identity also pursues
Jesus—from his entry into Jerusalem to the moment of
his death on Calvary. Who on earth is this man? How different the context of the question for Job and for Jesus
(see Matt 27:11–54; 21:1–11).

Maundy Thursday: Job 42:1–6, 7–17
Discovering What It Means to be Human
Job experiences the extremities of human agony and anger. He knows the tremor of God's overpowering voice. He
returns to the dust of his humanness (see also the comments on chap. 14) and awaits a new beginning from the
ashes. Like the rite of footwashing by Jesus, the act of in-
tercession by Job restores the community to oneness
before God. Saints have their humanness in common (see
John 13:1–17; 19:25–30).

Good Friday: Job 10:1–22
Condemned to Suffer
The saint who suffers unjustly may challenge the very
goodness of God. Job considers God's purpose in creating
humans an alien work. They are condemned to suffer even
before they are born. If creation necessarily leads to pain,
the incarnation leads to death. Job beholds the ugly side
of God when he suffers. The cry of the forsaken Christ on
the cross is only beautiful in retrospect. The passion of

Job challenges the goodness of God; the suffering of Christ redeems it (see John 18:1– 19:42; 19:1– 22).

Easter Day: Job 19:21– 29

Searching for a Redeemer

When their hope in this world fades, saints look to worlds beyond for deliverance. This passage is the climax of Job's search for a friend and redeemer (see also 9:25– 33; 16:15– 22). Job longs for someone to defend his integrity before the court of heaven, a redeemer who will vindicate him. Job knows of no resurrection after death (see comments on chap. 14); he looks for a redeemer of life. Jesus is a redeemer of a different order. He conquers death and makes life eternal for all humans, even Job (see John 20:1– 9; Matt 28:1– 10).

The Job Story:
A Gallery of Images
(Job 1:1– 2:13)

The story of Job is a traditional folktale about a pious patriarch from Edom. He belongs to the legendary world of antiquity, a sage like Noah, a hero who lives 140 years after his
ordeal (see Ezek 14:14). As a folktale the story of Job is not
concerned with reporting events in the history of Israel but
with exploring influential traditions of society. The pattern of
life rather than the course of events is central.

Perhaps the book of Job assumed its present form when
Israel was suffering the ignominy of exile. But we do not
know. The folktale as such (Job 1– 2; 42:7– 17) has its roots in
an era long before the day of the author of Job. The writer
adapts the old story to meet a crisis of faith he is facing. There
is no clear textual evidence to link this crisis with a specific
historical situation in Israel. The writer's concern is a meaningless life of suffering; his theme is universal. His prototype
may have been the Babylonian Job who suffered a similar de-
bacle until healed by the god Marduk through dreams and ritual acts.

As a folktale the story of Job is replete with images, motifs,
and traditional patterns. The events and figures of the narrative are balanced to create a good story. Job has exactly twice
the number of animals in his possession at the close of the
story as at the beginning. Four different disasters occur on the
same day to erase the four groups of living creatures in his
household. Yet Job survives to experience four generations of
progeny. The story is a vehicle for establishing a series of bold
images about God, human life, and personal destiny with
which the author is grappling. These haunting images are the
stuff of his tradition, the stumbling block of his faith, and the
grist for our sermons.

Images haunt our lives. Some are hidden in the attic of our
memory; others loom before us as seductive dreams. Some

are inherited archetypes; others are concocted as blueprints to boost our confidence. Were we to unpack these images and display them on the walls of our lives, they would present a formidable gallery. To walk that gallery would be to behold the legends we tell of ourselves. These images are more than ideas. They are visions that lure us, types that tempt us. The hiatus between the image and the ideal may leave us disappointed, lonely, or angry. Eventually we must come to terms with it. We may begin by unpacking the images and viewing them as part of our personal legend, the "once upon a time" of our own lives. To see those images for what they are—ideals, idols, or inspirations—is the second stage of the process.

The legend of Job is a gallery of images. The poem of Job which follows exposes the hiatus between legend and reality, idol and existence. Images drawn from the whirlpool of ancient Near Eastern mythology, international wisdom, and Israelite theology are all used to express the present form of the folktale. Portraits of the perfect patriarch and sage (1:1–5), Yahweh as an ancient court deity (1:6–12), disasters as celestial design (1:13–19), mortal life as interim (1:20–21), the saint as submissive human (2:1–10), and the friend as silent suffering companion (2:11–13), all hang in this gallery. The folktale collects these images and allows them to manipulate us through the medium of the narrative. We are caught up in the story and almost miss the subliminal way the images influence us. To unpack these images in the context of our own lives will be a major concern of this chapter. Each image will be a provocation for preaching Job within our modern world, a visual idea with which we will do combat to wrest the message from the text.

Preaching from the folktale of Job is typical of a particular preaching process in which an interplay between OT images and NT images is demanded. There is a tension between the OT portraits of the past, the radical images of the NT, and the popular ideas of our day. Creative interaction draws the listener into the struggle of faith: the preacher's search for meaning in ancient patterns of hope in the face of modern reality. Debate, struggle, and dialogue with the text are the order of the day. An overriding theme for a series of sermons on the prologue of Job would be "Unpacking the Popular Images of Our Faith."

A Portrait of Perfection (1:1–5)

The first image to be unpacked is a portrait of perfection. The storyteller draws together in one character the ideals of a noble man who "fears God," a hero of justice whose life is blameless, a prosperous patriarch like Abraham, and a legendary man of God. Job is the wise man *par excellence* (see Prov 3:1–18). He is perfect, the greatest in the ancient East. His public image is matched by a corresponding private piety. He sacrifices as the family priest, not because of any public misdemeanors or crimes, but because his children *may perhaps* have experienced evil thoughts in their hearts. He is more pious than the law demands. He is the image of a saint raised high above the level of ordinary humans. He is like Adam before the fall. He loves the Lord his God with all his heart, all his soul, and all his mind. He is too good to be true.

The advertising agencies of our time know well the power of traditional images for tempting the public. The immaculate woman executive, the congenial comfortable father, the super sports hero, or the sophisticated lover are all images of perfection that fall far short of reality. Job was the greatest, an example to be emulated. Preaching lends itself to using similar examples for Christians to follow. "Therefore be imitators of God," adds St. Paul (Eph 5:1). Well, we hardly go that far. God is a little too holy to emulate. Yet we seem to have created an image of the perfect Christian, a figure as idealized as Job the wise man. This ideal Christian is one with the idealized Jesus of legend, suffering calmly, turning the other cheek, heroic in faith, gentle in voice, and without a hint of guile or anger. Jesus would never have recognized his own portrait. To preach today is to unpack this image in the light of reality just as the poet unpacks the image of Job, the perfect wise man, and articulates his cries from the ashheap. The trail blazed by this poet offers us direction. To unpack the images of perfection that surround us is the beginning of self-understanding through sermons. The perfect wise man, the perfect Christian, the perfect mother, and the perfect leader are but a few of our idols. Perfect happiness is our common dream. The poet or the preacher must lead us from this gallery of images to the world of reality. There alone will we meet the God of Job or the Jesus of the Gospels.

One way in which these themes may be focused from the pulpit is offered in the following outline:

On Being Perfect:
      (a) The Folktale Job—Image of a Perfect Patriarch
      (b) Mr & Mrs America—Image of a Perfect Pair
      (c) Gentle Jesus—Image of a Perfect Christian
      (d) The Real Job—The Perfection Image Unpacked

Image of a Proud Deity (1:6 –12)

I am not a betting man, though I do not usually presume to condemn those who do. Yet I find it quite uncomfortable to meet the God of the Job legend making his wager with Satan. Perhaps the wager would have seemed less repulsive if it had not meant inflicting evil on an innocent victim. Who is this deity who makes deals with members of his heavenly court? Whence this awkward image of the Almighty? We live with a panorama of divine images, some from the OT, some from the NT, and some from contemporary artists of faith. Each claims our allegiance. Yet some are more compatible with modern tastes than others.

The portrait used to describe Yahweh as God in this folktale is not uncommon in ancient Near Eastern mythology. He is depicted as if he were the Ruler of a vast domain like the Persian Empire. His abode is a celestial palace with an entourage of courtiers, servants, and emissaries. He operates at a distance from his people on earth, using lesser heavenly beings as his agents of supervision. On a special occasion, probably at the annual heavenly New Year assembly above, timed to correspond with New Year festivities on earth, his court appears before him (1:6). The sons of God in this court seem to have diverse roles in the economy of their heavenly monarch. He, like the great Persian rulers, appears to have established a system of intelligence agents or spies who traverse the earth. Satan was one such agent. His assignment was apparently to search for signs of insurrection against Yahweh. In the OT, Satan is not yet viewed as himself the instigator of evil the way he is in later Christian theology. He appears before the court of heaven to present his findings and indict the guilty (see Zech 3:1 –2). He is, it seems, the prosecuting attorney of heaven.

Yahweh challenges Satan to indict Job, his perfect servant

on earth below. Satan responds by challenging Yahweh to ex-
amine the case of Job more closely. Satan contends that
Yahweh has smothered Job with blessings. Anyone would respond with piety under those conditions (1:9–11). God rises to
the bait. Let Job be inundated with evil, asserts the King, and
I bet he will continue to trust me (1:12). God is willing to allow
almost unlimited evil in order to win his case with Satan and
vindicate himself before the court of heaven. Job seems to be
but a pawn in this court game. But why the charade? Surely
the omniscient ruler knew the outcome of his wager. Surely
the God of heaven did not need to vindicate himself before his
courtiers. If the image of Job is that of a perfect man, the image of God is that of a rather insecure monarch. Or so it would
seem. Is this image from the folktale thrown up to highlight
the perfection of Job? In any case it stands in conflict with
other images of God, especially those of the NT. The Gospel
image of God forces us to judge the folktale image from Job.
All images must be appreciated in the light of the supreme image of God in Jesus Christ, whether they be the Warrior God
fighting the bloody battles of Israel (Ex 15), the Night Angel
wrestling with Jacob (Gen 32), Elohim creating the universe
by cosmic command (Gen 1), or Yahweh overcoming the primordial forces of chaos (Ps 74:12–14; Isa 27:1).

In the Gospel of John the image of God is that of an involved Father, not a proud monarch. The one sends his son,
the other sends spies. The Father's son suffers for other
humans in response to divine love. The monarch of the legend
forces a human being to suffer innocently to justify his divine
ego.

The God of the Joban tale seems to be a false image, the
kind of distorted picture we gain when we attempt to vindicate our images of human perfection at the expense of God. If,
for us, Job is perfect, then God must be imperfect beside him.
Such is the risk exposed by the motifs of the folktale. And such
is the possibility Job explores in his later tirades against his
God as the King of Chaos (see comments on 12:13–22).

Disaster by Design (1:13–19)

Atrocities and disasters have become commonplace. They
are part of our breakfast fare, the daily headlines, the space of
televised news. Plane crashes and national evils are so numer-

ous they remain impersonal spectacles until the day a messenger calls with the words, "I alone am escaped to tell you. This disaster is addressed to you. Death has come to your house."

Four times in one day the messengers arrived with the same words, "I alone am escaped to tell you." Four simultaneous calamities destroy Job's world. There had to be a reason, a design. Coincidences like that cannot be ignored, even by the most cynical.

Normally we would respond to disasters like those which befell Job in somewhat the following vein. The Sabean marauders who erased Job's pastoral ventures (1:15)—typical of those lawless elements on the margin of society. The flash fire from heaven (1:16)—obviously one of those freak electrical storms found in distant parts of the globe. The Chaldean bands who wrecked Job's commercial trading activities (1:17)—probably rebel forces that can be expected in unsettled parts of the world. The whirlwind that killed Job's family during their annual festivities (1:18 – 19)—clearly a hurricane or a tornado. It was "just one of those things."

Just one of those things! The folktale will not let us escape with that kind of contemporary folk theology. Four disasters announced on a single day! Just one of those things? Singly we could perhaps live with that popular explanation. Not so for Job. Someone has manipulated history and nature to focus the brunt of the ills on one man, the hero of wisdom and goodness. The culprit is clearly the proud God. Satan may have been the agent of God's design for Job, but the fire and the whirlwind are God's very own tools for destruction. It is explicitly "God's fire" which flashes from heaven.

The OT prophets and wisdom writers traditionally acknowledged Yahweh as the source of natural disasters. He controlled the whirlwinds, floods, and earthquakes. He effected the destruction of cities (Amos 3:6). Humans were often in the dark as to why disasters were sent, but ultimately he was responsible.

Job was more in the dark than most. He suffered not only one calamity but four. Yet he knew nothing about the court debate over his perfection. He knew nothing of the deal between Yahweh and Satan. He knew nothing of God's boast or the design to test his faith. Job was completely in the dark. The hidden God was keeping his design quite secret. When

Abraham's faith was tested, Isaac was ignorant of God's intentions. Such is the lot of the innocent victim in the world of legend.

When we are confronted by a hidden God in the story of our lives we too are tempted to suspect him of secret deals or covert wagers. How else could such atrocities be explained? How else can we handle the apparent evil design of it all? Then again, is Yahweh any better than the fickle ancient gods of old?

Or is the story a set-up? How easily we are tempted to suspect God of something less than perfection. The folktale lulls us into believing it is possible, especially if we side with Job. As the grand debate continues Job becomes even more convincing as he berates God for harassment and spying (see on 7:11–21). At first blush the book appears to be a brilliant exposure of God and his ways.

In the Interim: An Image of Life (1:20–21)

I have never particularly liked the image of life as a pilgrimage or myself as a pilgrim. This image, as with so many of our popular Christian images of life, suggests a negation of this life in the hope of something better. We are on the road to a more sacred place, the glorious goal of our tedious pilgrimage. We arc on the highway to heaven along the dangerous infested roadways of this life. "The world is very evil," is a line from one of our familiar hymns. "Heaven is my home" we echo in another. Between entering and leaving this world we are in alien territory. We will be lucky to escape with our souls. We prefer retirement in those mansions above to involvement with God here below. We opt for a Santa Claus in the sky rather than a suffering Christ on earth. We do not really want to face the presence or plans of God for this life. In short, pilgrims tend to prefer heaven to God.

Job seems to be echoing a variation of this motif when he asserts:

> Naked I came from my mother's womb
> and naked I shall return there.

The womb to which Job refers is the earth, Mother Earth. The earth is both his origin and end. He is born of dust like Adam. And to dust he will return. Earth is his mother and she will be his comfort in the tomb; she will accept him again. The grave will mean peace, relief, and comfort (see comments on 3:13 – 19). In the vein of ancient Near Eastern myths, Job is portrayed as viewing life as an interim, a passage from the womb to the tomb of Mother Earth.

In the interim, Job is in the hands of Yahweh. Between the moments of departure from and return to Mother Earth humans are subject to paternal protection and direction. Yahweh, be he generous or grudging, is the giver of good and evil (see 2:10). He allots the share for each human life. Ultimately the maternal forces of earth control life; in the interim paternal powers of heaven direct them.

The image of life as an interim segment of time may emphasize the ephemeral quality of our existence. But should that image dominate? Hinduism avoids the interim image by acknowledging an endless cycle of rebirths. Totemism posits a timeless continuity between the life principles of humans and nature. For Job the image was harsh. He knew of no resurrection or rebirth (see chap. 14); plants were more fortunate than humans in that respect. Life as a brief interim between womb and tomb was indeed real in his day—and remains so for many today.

The image of life we project is as important a feature of our theology (and preaching) as our image of God. The images are legion. Life is a game to be played, a time to win or lose. Life is a case at court or a struggle to survive. Life is a journey, a path to enlightenment, a river, a rat race, a bowl of cherries, a joke. Or, as a popular song expresses it, "In the meantime, in between time, ain't we got fun!" To clarify the precise image of life appropriate to the Gospel story requires serious thought.

The Gospel message of John and Paul transforms the image of life as an interim. We are in Christ *now;* we have eternal life *now;* we are sons of God *now*. We are alive to Life now . . . and to hell with Death. We celebrate the eucharistic banquet of the Lamb now. A sermon outline exploring this image may assume the following pattern.

In the Interim:
    (a) The Interim—an Image of Life
        Naked I came from my mother's womb
    (b) In the Interim—the Give and Take of Life
        The Lord gives and the Lord takes away

(c) Interrupting the Interim
   The Lord takes (Death) and the Lord gives (Life)
(d) Interims Unlimited
   The Comings of God—time and again

An Image of Capitulation (2:1–10)

I have always had a certain sympathy for Job's wife. She seems to be the only realist on the scene. Her advice to curse God would have put Job out of his misery and exposed Yahweh as the culprit. She is not concerned about God winning his wager with Satan. She is not inclined to treat God with kid gloves. Her plan is to let him have it between the eyes: he deserves it and Job deserves some relief. His death would be a mercy killing, sweet peace at the hand of a savage God (2:9).

To curse God in the ancient world meant to call down God's destructive wrath upon human life. And why not? What good was life for a man bereft of blessings and plagued with bodily ills? The court of heaven was called into session a second time. A second time Job becomes the victim of satanic ills. And a second time God lays bets on Job's fidelity (2:1–3). Why should Job avoid the advice of his wife? Why not curse God and die? Ironically, when Job does unleash his curses against God's plan for human life (in chap. 3), he does not relieve Job of his life. Rather, he increases the torment by refusing him death. In the world of the folktale the curse would have been final. But Job's patience is perfect. He accepts everything from God, good and evil . . . and it is all evil!

Contemporary popular responses to personal ills and public atrocities are neither that of Job nor that of his wife. More often the reaction today is, "How can there possibly be a God if he allows things like that to happen?" Evil in the world has become a prime excuse for denying the existence of God. That excuse is coupled with a false image of God that makes him little more than Santa Claus. He only does nice things, gives good gifts, and has nothing to do with evil in the world. That god is not God!

In Job God is taken seriously, deadly seriously. For he not only allows evil things to happen, he is somehow involved in their happening. There is no escaping him, even in the folktale. Accept his role in the ills of our lives or force him to erase us from beneath his rule. That is the import of the dialogue between Job and his bitter wife.

Job capitulates. He accepts the will of God and suffers in ignorance. Jesus Christ accepts the will of God as part of his plan of salvation and suffers knowingly. Yet even for God's son there was no relief. God did not come down to save Jesus from the cross. His agony was salutary, part of the cosmic plan to redeem life through death—an act of atonement. What redemptive value is there in the blind suffering of Job? His way was the path of meek capitulation; his wife's resolution was an easy answer. We learn the meaning of suffering when our own experience, our own story of anguish, is linked first with the story of Job and thereafter with that of Jesus Christ. We empathize with one and are liberated by the other.

Only when we move from the folktale to the poem, however, can we fully sympathize with Job; only when we move from the screaming Job of the poem to the silent man of Calvary does the full implication of God's involvement in the evils of the world begin to make sense. If, indeed, God can be portrayed as sending evils for Job, we must retort that he also sends his Son because of the evils of humanity, Job's included.

Job's wife has always suffered from bad press, a common plight of OT women. She, like Eve, or the loose woman of Proverbs 7, is seen as the great temptress. But is that true? Is not our image of people including biblical characters, governed by a stereotype that demands revision?

A sermon which could serve to interpret the attitude of Job's wife might illustrate her pragmatism as follows:

(1) She too has been bereaved when their children were killed;

(2) Her security has been threatened;

(3) Her husband's physical condition is repugnant.

Mrs. Job, as a practical woman, is ready to cash in. She assumes God has put all this misery upon them. Instead of doubting his existence she is ready to rail out at God, and is so full of her feeling that she tells her husband this is what he should do.

She stands there, tense and angry, ready to challenge God through Job. "If you've got any sense at all, Job, you'll curse God and die—that'll show him!"

Consider this text again and "Give Job's Wife Her Due."

(A) Curse God and Die!
  (1) Her suggestion is realistic, honest, unequivocal.
  (2) She is moved, it would seem, by a genuine sympathy for her husband; her honesty stands in sharp contrast to that of the three friends who are later rebuked by God; she is only rebuked by Job.
  (3) Later, Job follows her lead (chap. 3) and curses freely, if not precisely as she had hinted; he curses his birth and origins, and thereby indirectly accuses God.
  (4) Job is a pawn in the wager between God and Satan; Job is framed, trapped and ignorant of the demonic plot; by cursing God, Job would be forcing God to kill Job and lose face in the wager; Job's wife is implying that if God falls for such a wager he deserves to lose.
  (5) Any deals, wagers or commitments about serious matters deserve the kind of open honesty of Job's wife, not the hiddenness of Yahweh's plot.
(B) Why Maintain Your Integrity?
  (1) In this cry Job's wife presents the other side of her approach.
  (2) She is willing to compromise to teach God a lesson.
  (3) Job, however, refuses to deny his integrity, even in his curses; he maintains his innocence to the end (see 27:1–6).
  (4) Job, thereby, seems to expose God's compromising ways.
  (5) Job, like Jesus Christ on the cross or on the mount of temptation, refuses to compromise (see Matt 4:1–11).
  (6) In the end Job affirms his ashheap in spite of his friends, God and wife (42:1–6); his wife remains the most honest and creates a new family in spite of his rebuke.

The Art of Friendship (2:11–13)

If Job is portrayed in the image of an ideal wise man, a type of the perfect patriarch (1:1–5), then the three comforters of the folktale are comparable exemplars of the true friend. The image is subtle but significant. These men come from distant places when they hear of Job's crisis. They hail from obscure places like Shuah which seems to be associated with Edom (Gen 25:2). They leave all behind so as to be with their friend. Nothing else matters at that time. They come to comfort and sympathize, to exercise a particular ancient art they knew well. They identify with Job, perform ritual laments of empathy, and become one with him in dust and ashes. And, above all, for seven days they keep their mouths shut! Silence alone seems appropriate before such an awesome tragedy. In the poem which follows, these three friends are depicted in more realistic terms and are duly castigated for their verbosity and treachery (6:14–30). But within the story they are valuable portraits of an ideal friend, much like the image each of us hangs in the gallery of our lives.

The image of a true friend provokes a number of questions pertinent for preaching. Can a friend really identify with the suffering of someone else? Or do we, in the last analysis, suffer alone? The professional friends of our day could hardly survive if they identified too closely with their clients. The nurse, the doctor, the psychiatrist, or the social worker is confronted by a mass of Job figures looking for comfort. Preachers too, who are expected to double as friends, are pressured by the cries of the tormented. They preach love and sympathy, but cannot spend themselves totally by identifying with those in pain. They are supposed to be professional "lovers," friends with an apt word of comfort. Yet in seeking to touch others they themselves may become castaways. Surveys, in fact, have shown that few clergy have close friends in their congregations or even among fellow clergy. They are expected to be self-sufficient, professional friends—but with no friends of their own.

Perhaps the contemporary ideal is captured best in a song of Judy Collins:

> You're like a rainbow coming around the bend.
> And when I see you happy,
> Well, it sets my heart free.
> I want to be as good a friend to you
> As you have been to me.

Job's image of a friend is that of a loyal advocate in the day of total despair (see comment on 6:14). Friendship as exhibited

by the friends of the folktale is a specific art to be cultivated.
Perhaps that is where the parish can grow. We have been inundated with sermons and slogans about love, loving our
neighbors, loving our enemies, and so on. "They'll know we
are Christians by our love," we sing in pious harmony. Love
has become a slippery shibboleth. Loving is assumed to be
some natural impulse which rarely in fact erupts. Friendship,
however, is an art. Serious covenants of friendship between
people of God may produce far more response of human concern than all the glib exhortations of harried preachers to love
everyone.

    It is not insignificant that Jesus' command to "love one an-
other" is interpreted by John in concrete terms of obedience
and friendship. Jesus is the personal friend of his disciples
precisely because they have shared the secret of his relationship with the Father. Shared suffering, need, mystery, celebration, and life make friendship in Christ a realistic power
within the kingdom as it operates in the parish. A sermon and
perhaps a rite on "The Renewal of Friendship" is suggested by
this text. Broken friendships, a new covenant of friendship,
and the art of friendship in Christ are themes for such a sermon. Genuine friendship is rare (see the comments on 6:14–
30).

The Grueling Debate: Taking On God
(Job 3– 27)

"Thy will be done" has long been the response which Christians have been expected to utter in the face of disaster, doubt, or trouble. We seem to have been conditioned by Victorian ethics to be meek and mild in the face of God. The widespread image of a gentle Jesus has reinforced that anemic ideal. We are taught, it would seem, to be sweet children rather than mature adults before God. We are often viewed as "gutless" by the so-called real world if we claim to endorse that image.

The examples of Moses, Jeremiah, and Job belie the image. They take on God and wrestle with him. They are passionate protagonists. They refuse to let God escape without hearing the human side of the story, the agony of the earthly situation, and the fury of the faithful. They object to unreasonable actions of the Almighty and demand that he demonstrate his righteousness (see Ex 32:11– 14; Jer 15:15– 21). They take on God and refuse to release him until he responds, one way or another.

The example of Jacob is classic (Gen 32:22– 32). Caught unawares by the angel of the Lord in the night he wrestled until dawn. When the deadline came for God's departure, Jacob refused to release his opponent. "I will not let you go until you bless me," he replies. His blessing was a new name, a new identity. He was to be called Israel instead of the uncomplimentary name Jacob (meaning Deceiver). The title Israel was interpreted to mean that Jacob had taken on God and won. He had prevailed in a battle with God at a crisis point in his life and returned victorious.

Those of heroic faith have taken on God in similar vein. Job is a supreme example of such faith. He takes God seriously and refuses to let him escape from his onslaught of feelings, curses, accusations, and fury. He forces God to hear the human side of the situation, to know how it feels to suffer as an innocent victim at the hands of an apparently fickle deity.

He lets God taste the human emotions provoked by his arbitrary ways. The friends, who also come in for their share of
Job's castigation, are content to espouse those traditional doctrines which endorse penitent acceptance of the situation. The
Job of the poem is a man of integrity. He is not the image of
capitulation found in the folktale (chaps. 1–2). He refuses to
suppress his feelings of injustice, his ugly thoughts about God,
and his fierce opposition to the divine plan for his life.

The option of taking on God is also ours. How different parish life would be if our people took on God rather than meekly
accepting or blithely ignoring his involvement. And how
much more uncomfortable it would be for the preacher.

The great debate which rages in chapters 3–27 consists of
three cycles of speeches between Job and his three friends
(chaps. 4–14; 15–21; 22–27), with an opening tirade by Job
against pointless existence (chap. 3). There is a scholarly dispute about which of the speakers ought to be assigned sections
of the third cycle of speeches. Appropriate comments about
the position we have taken on this and similar controversial
questions are made at the relevant points in the commentary.

A few sections of three cycles of speeches have not been included for comment in this volume since they represent but
variations on themes discussed earlier. Within each of the sections treated we have often focused on pivotal verses such as
3:23 or 6:14 for expository consideration. These verses, however, are quite deliberately discussed within the context of the
appropriate section. Throughout, the major themes and issues
of the debate have been singled out for comment rather than
the patterns suggested by the three individual cycles
themselves.

A God Damned Birthday (3:1–12)

For Job birth was not accidental. Nor could he avoid it. It
was a date beyond his control fixed by celestial powers in an
appointed slot within the calendar of destinies. That was the
ostensible reason for his tirade of curses—that crucial un-
reachable moment in the past, his birthday!

We, like Job, invest great significance in pivotal moments
of our existence. Birthdays are among them, not merely because they mark the beginning of our physical transit from the
womb, but because, in some way, they seem to be momentous

for us in the pattern of destiny. Astrologers work on this principle and calculate the celestial import of our precise time of arrival. People today are Cancer or Virgo, Gemini or Aquarius. Their birth date is integral to their identity. For Job that date is damned. For us the appropriate sermon theme is "Times When We Deny Our Identity."

Job's curses are modeled on a reversal of the creation process. Traditional images of creation are negated in the rhetoric of his anger (see Jer 4:23–28). It is as though his birthday were Day One of creation. His cry can be paraphrased as follows:

> Let my birthday be damned (v. 3).
> Let there be darkness that day, not light (v. 4).
> Let there be an eclipse, not sunshine (v. 5).
> Let there be no Day One in my calendar,
> > no morning and evening of the first day
> > (v. 6).
> Let there be sterility (v. 7).
> Let there be Leviathan not Yahweh, chaos not order
> > (v. 8).
> Let there be no stars to soften the darkness (v. 9).

Christians have generally lost the art of sacred cursing. Not so Job! His string of imprecations would have warmed the hearts of Bluebeard's sailors. After seven days of silence in the company of his wise friends (2:11–13), the poet has Job exploding onto the scene with a vehement outcry of agony. While his curses are not aimed directly at God, they might as well be. They attack the sacred origins of Job's existence, holy beginnings that were in God's hands, not Job's (see the comment on 10:8–22). He, like Jeremiah (Jer 20:14–18), was not afraid to express in voluble language the fury within himself. . .and to direct it at God.

The cause of his fury becomes explicit in verse 10. The doors of the womb should have been closed and his mother (perhaps Mother Earth as in 1:21) remained forever pregnant to prevent a life such as his, an existence marked by "trouble." "Trouble" seems to be the key term. The Hebrew expression ('amal) has the import of unremitting oppressive trials. It is used of Israel's agonies in Egypt (Deut 26:7) and the sufferings of the Suffering Servant (Isa 53:11). In Job the term signifies that total package of misfortune, suffering, and ill that human flesh is heir to. It is summed up admirably in the Negro spiritual, "Nobody knows the trouble I've seen."

To be born, cries Job, is to be born a slave in a life of endless agony. Better not to have been born at all. Many of us, like Job, are ready to negate our identity by seeking escape in heaven, in self-pity, in suicide, or in wishful thinking. Perhaps Job had more reason than most of us. Yet I recall a woman with good cause. She was a friend in a city psychiatric ward. She had attempted suicide but refused to admit it. "No," she said, "I do not want to continue my life and I do not want to take it." Naively I replied, "What other option is there?" "Oh, that I had never been born," she said without hesitation.

For those *in extremis* the reversal of existence is a real option. For those who have endured persistent mental anguish there is no exit, no option. Only the past can be probed or, if possible, erased—from the very beginning. For these people the message of "No Birthday" is better than "Happy Birthday." They understand the plight of Job. When we would deny our identity, the experience of Job becomes real.

The 1970's have been dubbed the Me Decade. Personal identity was a central concern for many people through those years. They sought to discover the "true me" or the "real me" inside each of them. The assumption was that we smother our true identity. Job, it seems to me, offers a whole new perspective and points us to "A Faith Identity Crisis."

(A) Denying our Identity by saying "Nice Things"
    (1) Pious prayer that we do not really mean; assuming an image of concern when we could not give a rap.
    (2) Playing the role of a religious person when it is to our advantage—as some politicians do.

(B) Asserting our Identity by saying "Nasty Things"
    (1) Joining in jokes about gullible believers but denying our deep hidden faith.
    (2) Laughing at religion when it is fashionable; raising hell against the church to win a point.

(C) Asserting our Identity by attempting to deny our Identity
    (1) Job curses his origins and thereby his identity.
    (2) He attempts to stir the forces of chaos (Leviathan) and thereby oppose God's creative processes (3:8).

(3) Yet his curse is true to his agony, his feeling of identity at that time—he is honest to God.

(D) Finding a new Identity

(1) Job curses and Jesus is cursed—yet both have integrity.

(2) Jesus is cursed on a tree (Gal 3:10-14).

(3) He bears our curse; he exposes our false identities as hypocrites, like the Pharisees, deniers like Peter, or traitors like Judas.

(4) He offers us a new identity in him, blessed children of the Cursed One.

An Image of the Dead (3:13-19)

We may depict the world of the dead in gruesome terms to intimidate the impenitent or we may glorify its beauties to console the faithful. For most OT writers, the world of the dead is a vague shadowy realm of gloom with little to commend it. The land of Sheol is a region of darkness cut off from God's care (Ps 88:1-6). The dead are but shadows who laugh at the fallen great (Isa 14:9-11). The OT has no heaven above for the saints, only the womb of the earth where all may return to sleep (1:20; see comments on chap. 14).

Job's crisis, however, provokes him to idealize the realm of the dead. The grave is a refuge from the prying and brutality of God (7:21). Sheol is the welcome land of no-return (10:21-22). If Job could be concealed in Sheol and sheltered from God's attacks for just a little while—that would be heaven (14:13)! For Job the realm of the dead is inviting. It means relief from the "trouble" imposed by his God.

The image of an ideal world of the dead here in chapter 3 includes a long rest, plenty of sleep, escape from life's troubles, the company of kings, the absence of injustice, freedom from oppression, and absolute equality of slave and master. This land is a welcome world for those in torment and a far cry from the blazing hell of later apocalyptic writers such as Enoch. Job envisages this ideal underworld as the answer to his earthly problems. What of us? What kind of ideal worlds do we create, either in the future or the past, in heaven or in death, as unrealistic answers to our private "trouble." Where is our Eden, our land of escape? (See the comments on 1:20-21 and 7:1-10.)

Those who are called into the kingdom of God by Christ are not invited to escape the world but to take up a cross and follow him. He provides us with "An Alternative to the Alternative." There is no place or refuge, no Eden, no "beautiful isle of somewhere!" The disciple leaves his or her own "troubles" to enter the world with another burden, a liberating load, a message of deliverance from ultimate bondage. The disciple does not escape, but returns to the so-called "real world" with a new understanding, a new being. For Job there was, as yet, no invitation to life; he knew only the face of evil—and it looked very much like a creation of God.

What's It All About? (3:20–25)

What's it all about? What's it all mean? Time and again we pose that question when things are going wrong. The quest for meaning in life, for purpose in being or worth in our petty contribution to humanity is often seen as typical of contemporary Western malaise. We are confronted by aimless, rootless people wandering around asking themselves endless questions about why they are on this earth. "What's it all about?" That is a sermon theme of this text.

The quest and the question are not new. After Job's barrage of vitriolic curses in the face of God (3:1–12), he lashes out with vehement complaints about existence itself. In the background, one should see the lament Psalms punctuated with the liturgical "why" of anguish (Pss 10:1; 22:1). At the heart of his concern is the ancient wisdom symbol of the "way" (Hebrew derek).

According to Proverbs 4 there are two ways: the way of wisdom and the way of the wicked. Wisdom promises to be the guide, path, and goal for those who choose her way. Those who pursue the way of the wicked will lose their footing, stumble, and fall by the wayside. The ways of wisdom are secure and true, the path ahead is perfectly clear.

> The way of the righteous is like the light of dawn,
> which shines brighter and brighter until full day.
> The way of the wicked is like deep darkness,
> They do not know over what they stumble (Prov 4:18–19).

The way of folly takes one into the realms of death (Prov 9:13–

15). The way of wisdom leads in blazing sunshine to the tree of life, to wisdom herself in the midst of Eden (Prov 3:13–18). What more could anyone ask? Broad is the way and bright is the path that leads to wisdom.

Job has a different vision of reality, wisdom or no wisdom. Why should the sufferer, the one oppressed with "trouble" (see v. 10), ever be graced with life? (v. 20). What is the point of existence if life is bitter and death better (vv. 21–22)? Why persevere with giving humans life when they long for death? Why?

The ugliness of life for Job is not merely that life is a time of torment, but rather that we live in torment without a reason. The torment is meaningless. Even that could perhaps be tolerable, given sufficient palliatives. What makes life worse is that the intended meaning for life, the "way" has been hidden from us. There is a meaning in the torment but we do not know what it is. Even worse than that! The one who hides that meaning from us is God himself, the very one who should have shown us the point of life, in spite of our "troubles."

This message is wrapped up in Job's classic cry:

> Why should a man be born when his way is hidden,
> hedged in by God on every side (v. 23; translation
> mine).

The "way" is the meaning and direction of life. The hedge is that suffering which prevents us from finding the way. The ultimate cause of our blind wandering is God himself. Satan had accused God of fixing a hedge of blessing which prevented Job from facing reality. Now Job accuses God of revoking all his wisdom training had taught him. Given a hedge of evil, reality is meaningless, God a cruel delusion, and Lady Wisdom a lying harlot.

Suffering is harsh. Suffering without meaning is cruel. Suffering without meaning at the hands of one's God is sheer torment (v. 26). What's it all about? Job poses the question in all its pathos. In the struggle of the book he searches for answers. To dwell on that question in this context is the point of this passage. Without the struggle there is no answer for Job, for God or for us.

For some strange reason I have often experienced a minor depression during the week after Christmas. For weeks I join

family and friends in buying, celebrating and anticipating the
joy of sharing presents. Yet the rite of opening the presents
lasts for but a few minutes—and many of the toys do not last
much longer. How absurd! Hedged in by blessings for a day,
Satan would sneer. Take them away? What then? That week
after Christmas is like Job's affliction to me and his cry in 3:23
rings in my ears. What is the point of life? If it all ends in loss,
then it is absurd.

(A) The Absurdity of Existence in the Face of Mortality

    (1) Existentialists like Camus (in his *Myth of Sisyphus)*
maintain that modern humans see life as absurd.

    (2) If we come into existence only to be annihilated by
death, life loses its sense of meaning and becomes
absurd.

    (3) Why be born? Yes, echoes, Job, Why be born? Why
live?

    (4) To struggle heroically against the absurd, replies
Camus, to fight against death with all our might!

(B) The Absurdity of Existence in the Face of Suffering

    (1) The existentialists know only half the story, Job
would reply; for not only are we granted an existence that is terminal, but that existence is also
plagued by suffering.

    (2) In the torment of that suffering we can find no way
(derek) or purpose in living; why? because God, by
imposing suffering, hides the very "way" we are intended to know.

    (3) What can we do? Surrender to death *or* take on God
and struggle heroically against his absurd ways, replies Job.

(C) The Absurdity of God's Human Existence

    (1) The Incarnation is the act of God entering that very
existence we find absurd; he affirms our absurd
humanity.

    (2) He even participates in the death process which ap-
pears to make life meaningless; he assumes the way
of suffering to become totally human and know our
absurdity. The Innocent One dies on the cross as a
criminal. How absurd!

    (3) The path to life through death is the "way" now re-
vealed by God; we know it deeply in our struggle
with Job and Jesus.

The Man Who Should Have Known Better (4:1–9)

It is all very familiar to us. We live happily in our religious heritage for years. We revel in our rich sacred traditions for much of our life. Then suddenly something happens to challenge them. They no longer make sense the way they once did. Yet the community around us still speaks from the same traditional theology by which we once lived.

For Eliphaz, that was the traditional theology of reward and retribution typical of the wisdom school (Prov 4–6) or the theologians of Deuteronomy (Deut 7–11). In popular terms this wisdom theology is exemplified in proverbs such as "Honesty is the best policy" or "People who play with fire get their fingers burnt" (see Prov 6:27). In theological terms the message was that "The righteous will prosper and the wicked will be punished with various forms of suffering." In a context where there was no expectation of a corrective beyond death for the imbalances and injustices on earth, this principle of reward and retribution was expected to be operative in this life, not in some future world. The good were to be blessed and the bad cursed, here and now. When that process was delayed the Psalmists plied God with their laments (Pss 22; 69; 88).

A serious problem arose when that principle was viewed in terms of outcome rather than intention. When someone was prosperous, was he or she therefore righteous? When someone was suffering was he or she therefore guilty of some crime? Apparently when the known wicked persisted in their ways and continued to prosper, the righteous believed that one day their just God would catch up with the evildoers. It was merely a matter of time! When a specific individual fell into great distress or misfortune, it was not "just one of those things." It was a direct visitation from the Lord of justice, an act of divine punishment. There had to be a reason, and that reason was popularly interpreted as personal guilt. The idea of a wager between Yahweh and Satan suggested in the folktale (1:6–12) was not possible. God could not be that devious; the human being had to be the culprit.

Poor old Job, mutter his friends, he should have known better. He had spent his life preaching that same religion (4:6). He had comforted others with his wisdom teachings (4:2–4). It is sad to see him panic now that trouble reaches him (4:5). He knows the doctrine well: "Whatsoever a man

shall sow that shall he also reap." If he sows "trouble" then he
will reap "trouble" (4:8). And Job had admitted that oppressive "trouble" was his problem (see comments on 3:10). Innocent people do not perish (4:7). Poor perishing man, he must
realize he is guilty. Yes, poor fellow, he should have known
better.

How easily we fall into the same idiom and preach like
Eliphaz. Our line is similar today!

> He should have known better:
> He came from a good home and a good family.
> He had a good education and good parents.
> He had a good grounding in the faith.
> He knew the truth; he even preached the truth.

When we make such comments we betray our hypocrisy, the
assumption that deep down we really do know better. We assume that we are true to the tradition, the teaching of our
faith, or the Scriptures. He should have known better; he has
become a publican. We know better; we are the Pharisees. We
have the NT revelation. We would never act like Eliphaz to
another member of our community! Or would we?

On Having Nightmares about Theology (4:10–16)

Eliphaz was not given to excitability. He was a man of
discipline. He knew the traditions and stood by them. He
was an expert in wisdom theology. His teaching had been
closely scrutinized in the best wisdom methods of analysis
and tested among his peers (see 5:27). He was logical and ra-
tional, a pillar of the community. He had no need of personal revelations.

Yet in these verses he claims to have a special revelatory
experience. Is he serious? Or is this text in line with the sarcastic comments which are part of the rhetoric of rebuff (see 4:2)?
Is this passage a parody on those who, like Job, claim that revelation comes by personal experience rather than verified tradition? I believe so. First, because the language describing his
revelation experience involves rather deviant images and also
because the message of revelation he claims to receive is, in
fact, not a new revelation at all. It is a traditional wisdom axi-
om about human beings which appears in variant forms elsewhere in Job (15:14–16; 25:4–6).

As a parody the text is delightful. Two images dominate.

The first is a portrait of revelation by the word (*dabar*), a term used regularly by prophets such as Jeremiah (e.g., Jer 1:4; 2:1). Instead of the traditional idiom, "The word of the Lord came to me...," we read that the word steals into his ear like an insect and whispers a divine secret. Visions of the night were known to Daniel (Dan 2:19). The night visions of Eliphaz, however, are portrayed as nightmares during which the word slowly penetrates. The deep sleep he experiences is described with the same terms used to depict the primordial daze of Adam (Gen 2:21). Perhaps no rib was extracted from Eliphaz, but he experiences paroxysms of terror and great bodily seizures. He is a man possessed by the word, ranting and raving in the night. The second image is that of the spirit (*ruach*), a technical term used by Ezekiel and the ecstatic prophets to define the power which overwhelmed them (Ezek 2:2; 3:12–15). But the spirit does not enter Eliphaz; it brushes across his face like an apparition and makes his hair stand on end. It does not appear before him as the Angel of Yahweh or the glory of the Lord. Rather it assumes a mysterious shape, a ghostly form whispering words of theology.

The parody is perfect. The contention that revelation is mediated via traumatic personal experiences, like those of Job, is repudiated through rhetoric rather than dogma. The technique is part of the disputation style. It hits Job where it hurts. The truth he experiences in his pathos is personal. It can hardly stand up against the weight of ancient tradition. Even after Eliphaz has finished his revelation game, his theology by nightmare, he strikes again. His conclusion is a cold message that humans are mortals and that mortals are corrupt before God (see comment on 4:17–19).

It is easy to parody the ecstatics, the enthusiasts, the charismatics, or the existentialists. It is comfortable to put private revelations aside in favor of sober theology. Job would never have been heard if men like Eliphaz had had their way. Yet the unconventional and the eccentric is often closer to the kingdom than we think. Job's unorthodox experience of God as an inhuman foe is intensely personal. Yet it explores truth in a refreshingly honest manner that was alien to the doctrines of Eliphaz. I have found that oral faith histories of saints in the parish are themselves effective sermons, in spite of the parody of Eliphaz.

Humans in the Hierarchy of Corruption (4:17–19)

On three occasions Job's friends argue the case for Job's corruption as an inevitable outcome of his inherited human condition. The argument runs as follows:

> God the Creator above is pure.
> Creations of a higher order than humans are impure.
> Humans belong to a lower order of creation.
> Therefore humans are impure.

In the first version of this argument (4:17–19), a polarity is posited between God as Creator and humans as clay or dust. As dust humans belong to the earth, a lower component of the cosmos. Even creatures of a higher order, such as God's celestial messengers on high, are not free from guilt. Even they are not trustworthy. Human beings, then, have no right to assume anything other than impurity can emerge from the earth. Humans are by nature impure clay (see comments on 5:6–7).

Later Eliphaz argues that this corrupt nature is evident in the woman-born character of mortals (15:14–16). They are part of the corrupt birth processes of earth below. Human beings, he claims, are moved by a relentless compulsion to live by corruption and to feed on evil as their normal source of sustenance. Evil is integral to the human condition (see comments on chap. 15).

The third version of this argument contrasts celestial symbols with marks of human mortality (25:4–6). Moon and stars are compared with worms and maggots. If the former are imperfect, the latter must be putrid. Mortals are one with this putrid realm, the lowest order of creation, the domain of death itself. There is no way they can claim to be innocent. Instead of being a little less than the angels (Ps 8), man is little more than a maggot.

In this argument, the friends not only contend that human beings are sinners who have rebelled against God, but also, and more significantly, that their corruption is essential to their mortal nature. It is one with the dust of which they are made, a result of their birth from women creatures, a part of their close bond with the realms of death and disease. Mortality and decay are inevitable concomitants of guilt and evil propensity. The friends have a doctrine of original sin which goes beyond the Christian tradition of a rebellious impulse inherited from Adam. The traditional Christian interpretation of Genesis 3 does not render Adam corrupt by virtue of the clay from which he originated. He is not corrupt by virtue of his birth or origin. He is not corrupt because he associated with the ground—tilling the garden was part of his primordial task. Rather, his corruption resulted from a deliberate act of the will which alienated him from God (Romans 5).

A sermon on "The Nature of Human Nature" could begin with a look at popular ideologies which affirm humans as positive and good by nature and survey the other options. Behaviorists contend we are neutral by nature, a blank slate to be impressed by social patterns of good and evil. One traditional Christian liturgy reads, "we are by nature sinful and unclean." Is that text to be understood in the sense of Eliphaz or St. Paul? The Gnostic Christians of the early church viewed the body as totally corrupt, a prison for the soul, a dirty shell to be discarded. The Psalmist saw humans as created a little less than God, crowned with glory, honor and potential for greatness on earth (Ps 8). In this text, Eliphaz brings us back to an ancient theology. By virtue of our mortality we are infected with impurity. Can we accept Eliphaz' arguments?

The way we plan the education of our children in church or school will depend on whether we follow the theology of St. Paul, Eliphaz, the Psalmist, or a modern educator. . .or find some truth in all of them. That human beings have rebelled against God and stand in need of reconciliation is not the issue Eliphaz raises. The problem is the real nature of human nature and the degree to which corruption necessarily dominates our thinking and action. There is the crux for education. Eliphaz had but one message for Job: "You are totally corrupt by nature, so repent and submit to God's will." St. Paul responds that any who are in Christ are new creations (2 Cor 5:17). He also recognizes that humans, being both in Christ and in Adam possess an inner conflict (Rom 7). Our education, therefore, will always be a process in tension.

The Handicap of Being Human (5:1–7)

Eliphaz begins by throwing out a brief challenge for Job to find a celestial mediator from among the holy ones of the heavenly council to espouse his cause (vv. 1–2). Job takes up

Eliphaz' supposedly foolish idea and pursues it later (see comments on 9:32–35; 16:18–22; 19:23–29). Eliphaz gratuitously describes the ugly end he has known for fools like Job (vv. 3–5; see Prov 14:30). Here, as elsewhere, Eliphaz is really concerned with the question of what it means to be human (vv. 6–7; see comments on 4:17–19 and 15:1–6). The sermon theme on Eliphaz' lips is "The Sources of Our Suffering."

A poster appeared recently with two healthy children playing side by side, the one black, the other white. The caption read "Can you pick which of these two children is handicapped?" The implication was that the black child, though healthy, was handicapped by being born into an oppressive society where education and job opportunities would be less for it than for the white child. The sources of all such suffering are clear says Eliphaz.

(a) *We are one with the ground!* Eliphaz is alluding (in v. 6) to the story of Adam's fall. One of the curses of that fall are the thorns and thistles which now sprout from the ground (*adamah*) and make life a hardship (Gen 3:17–18). "Precisely!" says Eliphaz, "Does not affliction rise from the dust and trouble sprout from the ground (*adamah*)?" The ground itself is the source of our "trouble," the curses, pains, and cruelties of life. Humans are clay and no clay is immune from corruption. Humans are one with the earth and are obliged to experience the arduous trial of extracting a livelihood from the accursed ground. To be human is to suffer the curses bound up with our origins.

(b) *Our trouble is inherited!* Man is born to "trouble" (*'amal*), asserts Eliphaz (v. 7). The term man in the Hebrew is the word Adam. "Trouble" refers to that oppressive hardship and affliction of life against which Job had railed (see comments on 3:10). Those born of Adam are one with him; they are prone to suffering and oppression. It is not a matter of accident or circumstance. To be human is to experience the agonies of existence. For Eliphaz "trouble" is natural; we cannot avoid it. We inherit it with our birth.

(c) *Evil powers plague us!* Suffering is due to more than our human origins. Outside forces invade our lives and disease our bodies. The original Hebrew of the second line in v. 7 reads, "The sons of Resheph fly upward." Resheph was a deity of the underworld associated with disease and pestilence. Demonic forces, like the sons of Resheph, continually fly up from the underworld to corrupt human life. Regardless of how pure Job may be, he cannot escape his human origins or the impact of alien evil powers that bring him pain.

However we assess the ills associated with our humanness, the point of Eliphaz speech remains. We are born into a world where global corruption arises, whatever the source. We inherit a world with evils on an international scale. Famine, for instance, in an age of plenty is an international crime. Much of the earth's surface still produces thistles, not food. The ground remains cursed by the corruption of Adam, past and present.

When the Old Hymns Don't Help (5:8–16)

One of the gifts of good ministry is to speak the right word of God at the right time. Job's three friends are later denounced for not doing just that (42:7). Here, as often, their insensitivity is exposed. Eliphaz is quick to offer advice to the suffering Job. Perform the appropriate rituals of repentance (v. 8); then you will discover the mystery of God's ways (v. 9), and sing the doxology of his justice (vv. 10–16).

That was precisely Job's problem. The hymn to God's justice was the opposite of his personal experience. The lowly were not being set on high. The needy were not being saved from the hand of the mighty. The schemes of the wily were not being vitiated. Later Job responds with his own hymn, a hymn to the injustice of the King of Chaos (see comments on chap. 12). For Job the old hymns don't help!

The hymn which Eliphaz cites is a traditional wisdom hymn that paints everything in black and white. God saves the penitent poor and punishes the arrogant wicked. Through this reversal action of God, the believer discovers God's wisdom. Not so Job! For him God's ways remain unsearchable. Injustice still reigns. And God's ways remain unsearchable for many sufferers today! The usual advice to chalk our misfortunes up to the mystery of God is cruel counsel during the hour of personal agony. That was Zophar's mistake (see comments on chap. 11).

"Now thank we all our God," makes little sense when an

individual's world has been shattered by deaths or disasters.
It is tempting in such situations for the preacher to be an
Eliphaz, to say the right doctrine, to sing the approved song,
to be on God's side. God's side is not always that obvious.
"Don't be an Eliphaz!" is the topic that rises from this text.
Eliphaz would probably have said the same insensitive things
to Jesus on the cross when he, like Job, cried, "My God! My
God! Why hast thou forsaken me?"

I remember vividly the day my home burned. It was the
day before Christmas and in the dry heat of the Australian
summer the wooden farmhouse was consumed like tinder. As
we watched the blaze people came from everywhere. A pastor,
too, came—from wandering to and fro in the land. He put his
hand on my shoulder and said, "Norm, The Lord gives and the
Lord takes away!" I was angry; I wanted to hit him. There was
no comfort in those words at that moment. He was a comfort-
er like Eliphaz. The advice is serious: "Don't Be an Eliphaz!"
or "It's O.K. to Scream."

(A) At the bedside of the seriously ill

Eliphaz, with quick quotes on his lips, would probably
sing "Now Thank we All our God" in such a situation.
Accept the good with the bad; you've had a wonderful
life. Or, Accept your illness as a sign of your sins and repent. That is Eliphaz' way! The sufferer, however, may
need to scream, to confront the present as hell instead
of counting blessings or confessing sins! No thanks
God! It's not fair! may be their cry.

(B) At a time of personal tragedy

Eliphaz, with his easy grasp of God's mystery, would
probably sing "A Mighty Fortress is our God" at such
times. God has a good reason for such tragedies, says
Eliphaz. It's no good to us, cried friends of mine whose
son was killed the first day he saw action in Vietnam.
Where is God, the Mighty Fortress? A Mighty Fizzle!
That was their reaction, one we need to accept within
the community of faith.

(C) Before the Cross of Calvary

Eliphaz, with his penchant for logic, would have sung
"Onward Christian Soldiers" on Good Friday. If Jesus
were righteous, then God and his soldiers would surely
rescue him. "If God wants him, let him deliver him"

(Matt 27:43)! That is Eliphaz' line: God rescues the innocent and punishes the guilty!

Don't be an Eliphaz. The way of Job, rather than that of Eliphaz, points to the way of the cross, to suffering with those who suffer, screaming with those who scream bloody murder, and waiting with those who struggle with God to find an answer to the ills and tragedies of life.

Blessed are the Chastened (5:17–27)

Earlier in his speech Eliphaz had explored the corruption of human nature (4:17–19; 5:6–7). For him, suffering is synonymous with being human; "man is born to trouble!" (5:7). He does not, however, identify personal sin as the cause of Job's ill. There is no overt crime of which Job can be accused. He suggests, rather, that Job view his trials as the chastening work of God. Job should view his plight as a means of instruction, an education in the ways of the Almighty (see Prov 12:1). By means of this discipline, Job is being urged to submit to the Almighty and pray, "Thy will be done." If he surrenders he will experience the goodness of God and learn true humility.

The lesson Eliphaz hopes Job will learn can be summarized as a sermon outline:

Blessed are those who are chastened by the Almighty for they shall experience,
   (a) His healing power in their sickness (v. 18);
   (b) His saving power in their disasters (vv. 19–21); and
   (c) His rich blessings after their misfortunes (vv. 22–26).

A key point in Eliphaz' doctrine is the belief that for the penitent believer, disasters, ills, or misfortunes are not permanent or final. The Almighty, the Creator God of the patriarchs, is the Lord of life and death, good and ill, blessing and curse (see 2:10). In due course, all troubles will be overcome and wise believers will acknowledge their deliverance as a mighty act of God. The whole grueling experience will be a felicitous education in the wisdom of God. The faithful will appreciate how God distributes his blessings and redeems his people. Exultant believers will be able to laugh in the face of famine (v. 22). Not only is the Lord on their side, but they possess a covenant with nature herself which will, in the end, yield ample riches and prosperity.

Eliphaz' speech is tantamount to saying that all things work together for good to those who accept suffering as the chastening of God. Any sermon on the "blessed," however, needs to take into account comparable beatitudes in Proverbs (e.g. Prov 28:14) or the Sermon on the Mount (Matt 5:3–11). To be blessed is to stand in God's special favor even though suffering, persecution, or oppression would indicate the opposite to those unwise in the ways of God. If Job, contends Elihu, could but accept his tragedy as a sign of God's loving discipline, he would soon experience the beauty of God's saving grace. "Thy will be done" is the response Eliphaz expects from the lips of Job. Humble submission to the will of the Almighty is his path to restoration. In the speeches which follow Job explains why Eliphaz' counsel is laughable. It is God who needs to be taken down a peg or two. Job is completely innocent; he needs no chastening.

Hoping Against Hope (6:1–13)

The art of listening to the inner anguish of another human being is one of the most difficult skills to learn. Too often we either respond with trite and traditional answers or we sympathize on a surface level. We tend to hope the anguish can be covered quickly so that we can avoid looking on the bleeding wound at the core of someone else's being. We camouflage the soul in despair just as we hide death from public view. We want the agony to go away; it reminds us of our own mortality.

A sermon on "Listening to the Cry of Job" would force us to hear the ugly language of doubt, hopelessness, and spiritual exhaustion. An outline suggested by the text reads:

Can you hear me?
(a) When God hunts me down (v. 4);
(b) When nothing eases the pain (vv. 5–7);
(c) When I long to die (vv. 8–10); and
(d) When I have no strength to hope (vv. 11–13).

Several times Job accuses God of being a hunter who stalks Job as if he were a wild animal (7:20; 10:16; 19:22). Relentlessly he tracks down his prey and peppers him with poisoned arrows. Job is the innocent victim of this merciless heavenly archer. Frequently, like Job, for those in despair, God is the true enemy; he could have prevented their plight but chose to intensify it with an endless array of terrors (v. 4)

Those in pain need comfort, consolation, and sustenance if they are to survive. The proverb Job quotes is apt. A wild ass does not bray if he is well-fed. Job is not screaming just for the hell of it! (v. 5). Yet all the sustenance he receives is the tasteless pap offered by his friends (v. 6). All their fine doctrines and good intentions disgust him. Listening to the soul in despair may mean listening to someone reject our personal consolation and cherished counsel. Advice given from the comfortable context of our personal security is not heard. Can you hear? Those in despair may not want your old answers!

The ugly side of God the hunter is his cruelty to Job the animal. If God had any human feelings at all he would have put this wounded animal out of his misery (v. 9). Job's death wish is a plea that God would at least show a modicum of mercy to his harassed victim. Job could tolerate the pain if he had some assurance that God would finally make a decision and end it all (v. 10). In the cool grave he would find consolation. So often, the death wish of the despairing is real and the grave inviting. The empathetic listener sits at the graveside and views the inviting earth with the sufferer. To deny that reality is to deny the depth of that person's humanity. To affirm it is to be a friend (see comments on 6:14).

There comes a point in human suffering when the struggle to hope itself becomes hopeless. The inner resources of the tortured soul finally collapse. For Job there is no end in sight, no finishing line to sustain him (v. 11). He has no power left within his being to keep going (v. 13). At that point we almost hear Job crying to his God for help. But God is the persecutor not the savior, the enemy not the friend. His friends are no help and there is no "help" within him (v. 13). There is nothing but despair itself. "I get by with a little help from my friends," sang the Beatles. "Where are such friends?" Job queries.

Can you hear? cries Job. Can you hear me from your faith, Christian? Can you hear me from your comfort, friend? Can you hear me from your cross, Jesus Christ?

On Genuine Friendship (6:14–30)

The art of friendship was discussed in connection with
2:11–13. The three friends are supposed to be just that—
friends! They turn out to be more like traitors, in spite of their
compassion in the Joban folktale. Job indicts them for their
lack of genuine empathy and accuses them of personal treachery. They are like the wadis of Palestine that run dry in the
summer (vv. 15–20). They are fair weather friends of whom
Job has made no previous demands (vv. 21–23).

Job challenges his friends to be honest and say what they
are thinking. He urges them to specify precisely what sin he
has committed (v. 24). So far, he contends, their counsel has
been a barrage of worthless words. Their answers are not
blowing in the wind for Job to catch like butterflies. Their
words are wind! A man in despair knows when his companions are not being genuine in their replies. Job is not lying and
he demands the same forthright truthfulness from his friends.
Job's integrity is at stake (v. 29). He wants them to state openly what they think he has done to deserve his calamity (v. 30).

Until this point Eliphaz had spoken of Job's plight as the
inevitable outcome of being human (see comments on 4:17–
19; 5:1–7), or the happy chastening of the Almighty (see comments on 5:17–27). Now Job demands that his friends
pinpoint a crime in Job's past that is worthy of such tragic suffering. Genuine friendship calls for honesty in the hour of crisis, not some pious teaching or camouflage that avoids or
hides the issue.

One of the most powerful verses in the book of Job is 6:14, a
passage I prefer to translate,

> A despairing man needs the loyalty of a friend
> when he loses faith in the Almighty.

A friend is one who stands by us through thick and thin. Loyalty is the supreme mark of deep friendship. Regardless of the
consequences a true friend will stand the test of every trial. A
bond of covenant "loyalty" (hesed) sustains friends at a deep
spiritual level in times of despair. The extraordinary aspect of
this passage is the nature of the despair which is held up as the
test of genuine friendship. According to Job, one discovers a
true friend at the point where faith in God has been shattered.

One looks for a trustworthy fellow human being when God himself is no longer trusted. If God has become the enemy then a human being is needed as the friend. To be Job's friend means to be a fellow human with Job against the dehumanizing assaults of the Almighty. It implies empathy with the dust and ashes of Job's despair. And it involves taking sides with Job against God.

That kind of empathy, in Christian terms, means the way of the cross. To call Jesus a friend is not to claim him as a comfortable companion, but to accept his role as advocate on our behalf before God in the hour of despair. Jesus Christ knew the despair of Job in full measure. A sermon on friendship would summon us to be honest and empathetic in the terms Job specifies and Christ exemplifies. Later, when Job finds no human friend, he searches for a heavenly figure who will stand by his side before the court of God (see comments on 9:25–35; 16:18–22; 19:21–27; and especially 2:11–13).

I find it uncomfortable when preachers urge me glibly to love everyone, my neighbor, my colleagues, my enemies! Love is an easy word that becomes hollow when we try to spread it so thin! Perhaps Job is closer to the truth. We all have a "Yearning For Friendship." Genuine growth may lie more in building lasting friendships than in spreading love without commitment. We might develop this in a sermon as follows.

(A) The Loss of Close Friendships

    (1) Our contemporary society scatters people and hinders close bonds.

    (2) We experience a parade of fleeting contacts, a vast array of daily encounters and we tend to retreat from getting involved deeply.

    (3) Yet we are expected to be self-sufficient and independent; we are to be our own best friend, as the pop physchologists say.

    (4) We turn to professional "friends": doctors, social workers, clergy, psychiatrists.

(B) The Need for Human Friendship

    (1) Job cried for a friend who would be loyal at all costs, in spite of his outward appearance.

    (2) Job cried for someone to stand with him in his despair—and against God if need be! (v. 14 as translated above).

(3) Job needed a friend who could perform the role of a true friend with him—to listen, to feel, to suffer, to be honest, to scream at God, to wait—in short, someone who would be genuinely human with him.

(4) And such is our need in the face of rising anonymity and fragmentation in our society.

(C) The Option of a Deeper Friendship

(1) By committing ourselves to Christ as a "friend" before God we have a new option.

(2) His is not idle friendship; he has laid down his life for his friends.

(3) We have a commitment to sharing ourselves as human friends through Christ who shared himself in his life and passion.

(4) In Joban terms that means establishing a deep loyalty as honest, suffering, human friends of Christ at his table and in his Kingdom.

Escaping God (7.1–10)

Escapism is endemic to our modern society. Escape mechanisms enable us to avoid confronting death, age, evil, or deformity. Palliatives, sedatives, and diversions allow us to suppress the anxieties and traumas of life. Ways of escaping the reality of God in all his ambiguity and justice are likewise in evidence. Yoga, transcendental meditation, pop psychology and similar promises of inner peace and self-sufficiency abound. A popular book entitled *How to be Your Own Best Friend* offered a few simple psychological rules for achieving confidence, self-assurance, and success. To be one's own friend is to be at peace.

Job knew no such peace and no escape route. His fierce cry of agony may differ from ours, but his longing for escape has a familiar ring.

Oh, that I might escape God because:
(a) Life is slavery (vv. 1–2);
(b) Living is agony (vv. 3–6);
(c) And in death I would be free (vv. 7–10).

Job bases his rationale for escape on an ancient Near Eastern belief that human beings were created to be the servants of the gods. In order to liberate the overworked deities from

the tedious chores of temple service and the administration of
mundane affairs on earth, human beings were created as la-
borers in their place. "Hard service" in this text refers to the
forced labor typical under ancient monarchs (see 1 Kings
9:15–22). If that is the role and destiny of humans, asserts Job,
they will be slaves throughout their lifetime. Life itself means
labor and slavery; death means freedom and rest in the shade
(v. 2).

One of the most inviting features of the underworld is the
freedom the slave enjoys from his master. In Sheol, there is no
oppression; all human beings are equal (see the comments on
3:13–19). One can, of course, look for escape in sleep or loss of
consciousness. For Job that ploy was useless. The repulsive
diseases which plagued his body (v. 5) and the futility which
distressed his soul only served to heighten his consciousness
of reality as oppressive. His were nights of "misery" (v. 3), or
as the term is translated elsewhere, "trouble" ('amal, 3:10).
Oppressive afflictions had invaded his bed. He tossed and
turned through the night longing for the dawn (v. 4). But in
the morning he faced a fleeting life without hope or meaning
(v. 6; cf. vv. 13–14). God was the problem, the source of Job's
futile existence. Non-existence appeared to be the only escape.

It is difficult for the most of us to discuss death seriously or
face its reality even within a religion where an afterlife is affirmed. To invite death, as Job does, in a belief system where
there is no assurance of a resurrection to eternal life seems un-
thinkable (see comments on chap. 14 and 3:13–19). Yet the in-
tensity of Job's longing to escape God is so great that he finds
the land of death a tantalizing paradise (see vv. 14–17). He
even revels in the thought that God will not be able to find Job
on earth to spy on him. Job will no longer be around for the
eye of God to get a bead on him (v. 8). Job's life is short, after
all (v. 7), and soon he will have travelled to the land of no-return (v. 10), far from any place where the bothersome Almighty can inflict his pain on suffering humanity.

Such an escape would be delicious for Job; God would be
bereft of his victim. Why not commit suicide as Job's wife suggested, and take the final step of freeing oneself from the
clutches of God? Why not snatch life from the jaws of God and
die? Yet for all his yearning to escape, there is something
more important for Job than eluding God, namely con-

fronting God with the question of Job's own integrity. That is
the issue he tackles in the following chapters of the book. He
demands a trial to vindicate his innocence.

What Is Man that You Harass Him? (7:11–21)

Job's arguments in the preceding verses (7:1–10) would
seem to dictate suicide as the resolution of Job's tragic plight.
Job, however, has more than escape from despair on his heart.
On the one hand, he hopes to vindicate his integrity before the
Judge of heaven; on the other, he wants God to be taken to
task for his arbitrary divine acts. He demands that God ex-
plain why he selected Job for his inhumane assaults. The
themes of his complaint can be summarized as follows:

> Why single me out for harassment?
>   (a) Why treat me like a dangerous monster?
>   (b) Why bother harassing a human?
>   (c) Why prevent me from finding relief?

Job refuses to lie down and die. In his anguish he continues
to scream for an answer (v. 11). He is not some mythic monster like Yam or Leviathan whom Baal conquered in antiquity
or Yahweh subdued at creation (Pss 74:12–14; 89:9–10). Yam,
the Hebrew term for "sea" in verse 12, is the symbol of primordial chaos, like Behemoth and Leviathan in chapters 40–
41. Yam stands for those destructive forces which still
threaten to overwhelm the ordered world. But Yahweh once
placed them under guard, forever (Ps 89:9–10). Why should
God treat Job like a chaos monster? Amid the pains of his despair Job again looks for some relief, but none is forthcoming
(vv. 13–15).

According to Psalm 8, humans were created to be magnificent beings. They were appointed to rule God's world, to be
crowned with "honor and glory," and to be attended by special divine favors. According to Job, the Psalmist has his theology all wrong. Instead of God's special attention being a
"visit" that glorifies Job as a magnificent human, it proves to
be a "test," a relentless harassment which prevents Job from
catching his breath or swallowing his spit (vv. 17–19). Instead
of Job being created a little less than God as Yahweh had
promised (Ps 8:5), Job is little more than a wild animal, a creature in God's game reserve, a marked fugitive in the sights of

the hunter (v. 29). The harassment all seems so pointless. So Job voices his cry of disgust. If there is a sin which this violent God thinks I have committed why does he not reveal his loving side and forgive me instead of badgering me to death (v. 21)? What earthly reason does the Almighty have for hounding a miserable mortal? Why not forgive me and get it over with? Anyway, says Job, with a touch of humor in his words, I will soon be dead and then you will be frustrated, God, searching the earth for your favorite victim to harass. I will not be available for you to badger any more. I will be dead! I will be free! (v. 21).

The following sermon synopsis illustrates the way Job relates to the traditions of his own past (Ps 8) and the way we might relate to Job and to God in a dialogue of faith.

THE BATTERED IMAGE

When my father was sixteen he entered a boxing competition at a local fair. There he defeated several seasoned fighters, much older than himself. He won a medal and took it home to show it proudly to his parents. They were shocked and demanded he amend his worldly ways or they would bring the pastor to control him. Thereafter my father, like Job, had a battered image of his potential as a human being. Yet through that incident his humanness was given a new form. What of Job? His answer is in the text: 7:17–18.

(A) What Is A Human Being? A Battered Image?

> What is man that you exalt him,
>   and give him your attention?
> And you visit him each morning
>   only to test him every minute?

Heresy? Job takes the beautiful words of Ps 8:4–6 and changes them to fit his mood! According to Ps 8 humans are made a little less than God, creatures in the image of God, honoured as if they were gods set to rule the earth.

No so! cries Job. From where I stand—or rather, sit among the ashes—a human is a battered image. God exalts humans so that he can harass them, batter them, visit them with ills and test them with traumas.

God does not let Job live up to his potential as a human be-

ing in the image of God! God is the great frustrator! The great
watcher of humans (vv. 8, 20)! God seems to be an enemy at-
tacking Job (v. 20; 6:4). One would think, says Job, that I was a
chaos monster rather than one of God's special images. I am
treated as a threat to God rather than a protege!

> Am I Yam (Sea) or Tannin (Chaos Monster),
> that you set a guard around me? (7:12).

Humans have the potential to be God's representatives on
earth but, according to Job, God does his best to frustrate that
potential. God does not give us a high place, an image to be
adored! He sets us up as targets! We are battered images!
When my image is finally shattered, cries Job, it will be reduced to dust. Job keeps shoving in God's face the way he
keeps battering, battering and battering Job. "I don't even
have time to swallow my spit," he yells (v. 19).

Job closes this chapter on a note of ironic glee. The day is
coming, he retorts, when I will be dead—back in the dust.
Then, God, you will look for me everywhere, you will search
high and low for your favorite victim, but—wait for it, God—I
will not be! I won't be around for you to batter anymore! Then
you will be the frustrated one!

The fact that God would seek Job is a sign of an ambiguous
love-hate kind of relationship which Job feels. Later Job reminds God that he molded Job as a precious vase, a delicate
image (10:9). But when the precious is broken and the image
battered, how do we reply? How do we handle Job's words?

(B) Who Is This Human Being, This Battered Image?

We can respond to Job by saying he is excessive. We could
even accuse him of a sin close to blasphemy. We can ignore
him, and similar people in pain, people locked in homes, insti-
tutions, and attics. Or, we can cover these cries, including
Job's, with muzak, smother their pain with cosmetics and gar-
nish their world with sweet tidbits of soothing tradition.

Neither Jesus nor Job, however, were silent about their agony. Job takes his battering seriously, and, above all, he takes
God seriously—in fact, he takes it out on God. He tells him just
exactly what it is like to be human, just exactly what it is like
to be treated as a monster, a target and the butt of divine
ridicule.

Do you have any idea what it is like to be a battered image? Do you know what it feels like to be human, broken and torn?

As a matter of fact, I do, replies God! Hast thou considered my servant, Jesus? Have you seen his battered image? That is my image they battered, my precious son they set up as a target. That is my boy they treated as an evil monster, a criminal, a threat to their world. Oh, yes, I know what it is like to be human—in Jesus, and in you!

They put that battered image in the dust; they buried it in an earthly grave. And then—and this may surprise you Job—I sought him again. I sought him, found him, and raised him to life. I raised him to be vindicated, glorified and exalted as Lord. He stood upon the dust, a Redeemer like the one about which you dreamed, Job (19:25–26).

To me, continues God in the spirit of the Gospel, his battered image was beautiful. In the sixteenth century, in Japan, persecuted Christians were forced to step on an image of Jesus' face. That battered image was also beautiful. Yes, I allowed my son to be battered by sins and sinners. Yet, he bore their wrongs in his dying. And when he was exalted people began to understand and to believe in my plan, my Gospel plan, of life through death!

And God continues his message to us. I accept your screams, Job, friend, Christian young and old! I accept your battering and affirm you in your pain. I would not soften your cries, or refute your theology—I would only show you my face, not from a whirlwind but from a wooden post where my image is nailed, battered and beautiful.

Yes, I will seek you when you go to the grave, Job, just as I sought my Son. I will hear your cries from the dust, human sufferer, just as I heard my human child at Calvary.

Bildad's Solution to Job's Problem (8)

Bildad was a perceptive elder; he knew well the normative traditions of wise men in his day and realized the frightening implications of Job's accusations. If God were an inhuman heavenly hunter pursuing innocent earthly victims, as Job contended, then the Almighty was not a God of justice at all (v. 3). God's justice was the foundation of cosmic and human order. If God himself could commit atrocities then the universe was morally bankrupt; his righteousness and justice are the pillars of world order (see Ps 89:14).

Like Eliphaz, Bildad was willing initially to grant Job personally the benefit of the doubt and to focus the question of guilt on Job's children (v. 4). After all, Job had himself implied their sinfulness when he performed appropriate rites to expiate their possible guilt during their hour of festivity (1:5). The obvious solution according to Bildad was a simple rite. If Job were to serve as priest and intercede for his children again, all would be well. If Job would but throw himself on the mercy of the Almighty the whole crisis would vanish and Job's fortunes would be restored (vv. 5–7).

Bildad's advice is to "take it to the Lord in prayer." Penitent supplication is seen as the simple solution to a complex crisis; by performing the appropriate rite of reconciliation the *status quo* will be restored. The issue for Job, however, is not the answer to a specific prayer but the question of ultimate meaning in a life mutilated by horrendous agonies. That question was a quest not a simple riddle or petition. Job was searching for the place of God in his world. Such a quest does not end with morning Matins.

Job, moreover, wanted an investigation into God's treatment of his servant. He demanded a celestial commission to indict the Almighty, to challenge his justice and to vindicate Job. The issues were cosmic in proportion. No meek petition could resolve them. Faith may be able to move mountains if God is on your side; when doubt about God's integrity is involved pious prayers of faith may not be the answer.

A sermon on "The Limits of Ordinary Prayer" would enable the struggling believer to tackle the real doubts of life anew and to follow the alternative ways suggested by Job in the quest for understanding. Job "takes on God" rather than taking his petitions to God. He confronts and challenges God. He does battle with his enemy, his accuser, and his judge. For Job this is no ritual act but a life and death struggle. Yet, ironically, it is a form of prayer. His screams follow the pattern of vehement protest typical of Moses and Jeremiah (see Ex 32:11–14). Job is a righteous rebel demanding justice.

For Job, traditional prayer was futile. He wanted more than a one-way conversation with his God in heaven. He demanded a face to face encounter, a public court where he could tackle the Almighty in person and prove his case against God. He wanted God to come out of hiding and account for his actions (see comments on chap. 9). For Bildad, and for most of us, the ordinary means God has provided for communication with him are considered adequate. Confession, petition, absolution, and praise are part of the discipline of good worship. Job, however, was not about to admit his guilt and acquiesce in blind faith. He did not trust God to move the mountain of his ills.

Bildad's advice was not merely a personal opinion. He knew the tradition of the elders. "Consider what the fathers have found" (v. 8). Their counsel had stood the test of time (vv. 9– 10). Their message is based on a simple analogy: humans like plants need continued sustenance to survive (vv. 11– 12). Human beings who do not maintain close communion with God by following the established paths of wisdom meet disaster (vv. 13– 19). Job can be assured that if he is blameless, as he contends, the Almighty will not reject him (vv. 20– 22).

In the end Bildad is right; Job is affirmed by the Almighty. That affirmation, however, is born of Job's passionate struggle with the meaning of life amid the chaos of despair. No ordinary prayer led to Job's new consciousness of God (see the comments on 42:1– 6). Rather it was a relentless battle with God, an honest struggle with him about every doubt, fear and animosity he experienced.

The Problem of God's Power (9:1– 24)

The almighty power of God is normally a source of confidence for the faithful. Yahweh is stronger than all the gods of Egypt. "The Lord is the stronghold of my life, of whom shall I be afraid?" cries the Psalmist (Ps 27:1). Jesus could say with assurance that "with God all things are possible" (Mark 10:17). The power of God is assumed to be the arm of his goodness and justice. He can execute his noble plans of salvation.

For Job, God's strength was a problem. Because the Almighty was so mighty Job did not have the power to force God from his celestial refuge and drag him into court. Job wanted a court case where he could be publicly vindicated. "Can a man be just before God?" he cries. Or, in a preferable translation, "Can a man win his case before God?" (v. 2). The obvious answer is No! The problem, according to Job, is God's might.

Humans cannot make him leave his comfortable quarters and tackle an irate servant whose rights have been violated. A sermon on the uncomfortable ways God exhibits his power can be explored in this text of Job's outrage. The NT counterpoint is the ultimate way God used his power in the victory of Christ.

How does God demonstrate his might? By leaving humans with a barrage of unanswerable questions; a tactic illustrated when God spoke from the whirlwind (v. 3)! By violent acts of disturbance in the cosmic order (vv. 5–8) to balance his deeds of creation (vv. 9–10)! He is the Lord of earthquakes and eclipses, the storm God of old. He is the ancient warrior deity who "trampled the back of the sea dragon" (see the RSV footnote to v. 8) and crushed the helpers of the chaos monster Rahab (v. 13). Job's God is renowned for his great battles with the primordial powers of destruction. Yam, the unruly primal sea (v. 8; see 7:12) and Leviathan, the chaos monster like Rahab, are forces which God overwhelmed to establish the order of creation at the beginning of time (Pss 74:12–14; 89:9–10).

Job would suffer the same fate, presumably, if he took on God. He is too strong for humans to tackle, if he could be caught. Job, alas, cannot catch him. He is invisible, elusive, and inscrutable as he wends his violent way through the earth (vv. 11–12). When the power of God is linked with the hiddenness of a war God on the rampage, all justice seems to be vitiated. Such is the God experienced by Job as the innocent victim of divine harassment (see comments on 7:11–21).

Suppose this God were to grant Job a trial, how would he fare? How would Job tackle such a deity in court? From the outset Job would be at a disadvantage even though he is innocent. The evidence is stacked against him. He would be forced to assume the posture of the guilty party because of his pathetic condition. He would be obliged to address God as if he were the accuser. But Job wants the roles reversed (vv. 14–15). He wants to challenge God's actions and vindicate his human integrity.

Suppose, further, that God actually spoke to the court, what would he say? Whatever he chooses! Job does not believe that God would listen to his human voice (v. 16). He has no faith in God to answer such questions. The Almighty is more interested in abusing Job than conducting a fair trial. God is just as likely to smash Job with a whirlwind and render him silent (v. 17; see 38:1), exhausted, and bitter (v. 18). The power of God renders any court of justice between him and humans a farce. Job can never be vindicated while his God uses his might to silence his accuser.

Job's complaint about the power of the Almighty is restated boldly in v. 19:

> If it is a contest of strength, behold him!
> If it is a matter of justice, who can summon him?

Either way, Job loses. He has neither the power to fight God openly nor the authority to force him into court (see the comment on vv. 32–33). By misusing his power, God renders the moral order of the universe laughable. Though innocent, Job is made to appear perverse; the guilty, meanwhile, inherit the earth (vv. 21–24). Despair is the only conclusion, or so it would seem. What else is possible when God's alien power is in the wrong hands—God's!

At Calvary the power of God was also hidden. The innocent Jesus of Nazareth was crucified, abused and ridiculed. God did not step out from the clouds to vindicate his Son. There is no victory to silence the critics. Job demanded a trial and was met with a theophany. The sceptics at Calvary demanded a theophany and were surprised by a resurrection. God's power will always remain a problem for those who want God to use it to prove something, whether it be his justice or their innocence, his very existence or their goodness.

In the past I have written Litanies of Anger and Intercessions of Indignation. My friends have rebuked me. To endorse anger, they said, is to foster rebellion and hinder the virtue of Christian resignation. Perhaps they are right! But I appeal to Job, the rebellious saint, as my mentor. He is both saint and rebel, and in his honor it seems fitting to preach a sermon: "Affirming Job's Anger."

(A) In His Anger He Takes God Seriously

    (1) When faced with a tragedy many today reply by questioning the very existence of God; "a loving God would never let something like that happen!"

    (2) Job, however, expresses his anger, confronts God directly, and exposes God's deeds for what they are to humans.

    (3) Christians seem to have forgotten how to get angry with God; by suppressing their anger their faith has been stunted.

(B) By His Anger He Exposes Injustice
   (1) Job focuses directly on the injustice he has experienced and demands redress.
   (2) Job's cries point to Jesus' actions in exposing hypocrisy and corruption; Jesus emotions were hardly tame in the cleansing of the temple!
   (3) Job's anger also points to the righteous anger of people like Martin Luther King in their struggle for justice.
(C) Through His Anger He Achieves a Spiritual Catharsis
   (1) Job's self-understanding and his faith relationship with his God is transformed through his fierce struggle.
   (2) Our struggle with God, and indeed with Christ, may include similar expressions of serious passion.
   (3) Our daily renewal is not necessarily achieved through placid prayer or quiet meditation; anger in Christ can also be healing.

The Search for a Mediator (9:25–35)

On three different occasions Job longs for a mediator who will espouse his case and handle his conflict with God (9:32–34; 16:18–22; 19:23–29). This figure is variously called a mediator, intercessor, umpire, witness, friend, and redeemer. Job had previously denounced his three companions as fair weather friends who could not fulfill their assigned roles (see comments on 6:14). Now he looks beyond earthly support to the council of heaven. Perhaps there is a genuine friend above.

Job's major concern in chapter 9 has been the problem of God's mighty power. Job has neither the strength nor the authority to force God into court to conduct a trial, futile as that exercise would probably be. Job's efforts to mask his anguish prove futile; he cannot put on a good front. His mutilated appearance condemns him as guilty no matter what camouflage he uses (vv. 25–29). His attempts to purge himself of incriminating evidence are rendered useless by the sadistic impulses of God, who plunges Job deep into the mire. He covers Job with sores, sicknesses, and tragedies that mark him as corrupt. In the court of Job's day, such signs spelled guilt. Sufferings were evidence of an ugly crime or a life of sin. No one would believe that God was the culprit (vv. 30–31).

Job needs an influential figure who is not bound by normal human limitations. This figure would be sympathetic to Job's plight and capable of bringing his case to court. This umpire would have the authority to arbitrate between the contending parties and grant Job a fair hearing (v. 33). But until some such higher power can remove the intimidating rod of God from the back of his earthly victim no such justice is possible (vv. 34–35). Alas, it seems that no such mediator is available to Job. God always wins!

Who is this umpire Job longs to summon? The text suggests a celestial being such as the angel of the Lord who has the capacity or influence to handle God in court (see Zech 3:1–5). Satan apparently had the power to convince God that Job should be tested with calamities. In the council of heaven, it seems, God can be influenced (1:6–12). "Behold, all that he has is in your power," says the Lord to Satan. Job seeks a comparable show of power on his behalf, a mediator who can handle God in another heavenly court. If Satan is the accuser against men, there ought to be a corresponding advocate!

A sermon contrasting the mediator Job sought and Jesus the Mediator could highlight the radical nature of Jesus' role and clarify the differences between them. Job's mediator is summoned by Job, Jesus is sent by God. Job's mediator is to assume Job's cause and vindicate his integrity before God. Job claims to be innocent of any crime worthy of such a tragedy. Jesus mediates by assuming the guilt of the believer in the presence of a righteous God. Job's mediator forces God to face the injustice of Job's situation. Jesus moves God to accept the unjust by virtue of the cross, the redemptive deed of Calvary. Jesus placates an angry God, alienated by sin. Job's redeemer handles an angry man, alienated from God.

This comparison offers a traditional pattern of opposites. But is Jesus Christ the mediator any less accessible to the angry of our community? Is he any less available when the frustrated, furious, and broken need an advocate? Is he any less sympathetic when men and women like Job come with the terrors of injustice ringing in their ears? After all, he does understand the nature of innocent suffering!

The Problem of God's Goodness (10)

In the previous chapter Job struggled with the question of God's arbitrary power and the need for a mighty mediator to resolve his conflict with the Almighty. Job himself has neither the power nor the authority to force God to appear in court and provide an opportunity for Job to vindicate his integrity. In this chapter Job focuses on the problem of the Creator's hidden goodness. His opening sarcastic outburst is an assertion that either God is a heartless deity who despises the humans he creates or he is himself as finite a being as Job. In Job's experience, at least, the action of God is as fickle as that of a human (vv. 1–7).

Job's exploration of the goodness of God commences with a poetic portrait of the gentle individual attention God exhibited when Job was created. Job had once experienced the tender loving care of this divine artisan. God had once shown the steadfast love (*hesed*) that Job expected of a friend (v. 12; see comments on 6:14). Now Job attempts to stir the inner concern of God for his special creation by forcefully reminding him of his past love for this work of art (vv. 8–12). Like Moses, Job forces God to take account of his past goodness and promises (Num 14:15) in his future actions. But God apparently suppresses his loving kindness.

Seemingly God's goodness was a facade; his creative delight a game. For God had a hidden purpose in forming Job, a divine plan to provide for himself a fugitive to hunt down like a lion. The excuse for pursuing him was his apparent guilt (vv. 12–17). God's goodness is nowhere evident to Job. He is afflicted and marked by God as guilty. God shows him no mercy, eases none of his pain, softens none of his woe. Rather he intensifies his attacks on Job and with each onslaught Job appears more guilty. Each additional suffering is a witness against him. All the goodness of God as creator is nullified by his inhuman harassment of this weak human creature (see comments on 7:11–21).

Job's existential question is paramount. Why does God spend such loving energy on his human creation only to treat him like dirt? Why does he bring human beings into the world if suffering is their appointed lot and anguish their destiny? Why does God badger his little human creatures? To be still-born is a better fate than life with such a God (vv. 18–19; see comments on 3:11–16). Without the goodness of God life is pointless. If God has any heart at all he will ease his persecution of Job and grant him comfort in the grave (vv. 20–22).

Nowhere is the juxtaposition between God's goodness and his apparent ugliness more sharply presented in Job. The gentle potter becomes the demonic hunter; the creator is the destroyer. The appropriate sermon for this situation is found in Job's technique of "Reminding God of the Beautiful." Like Moses, Joshua and Abraham before him, Job dwells on God's goodness to provoke his mercy. He tries to evoke divine empathy by recounting the delicate work of the Creator. There he invested his love; he created a beautiful work of art, a human being. When God appears ugly, when his purposes seem demonic, when his ways seem contrary, when his actions seem unfair, remind him of the beautiful! Remind him of his promises to forgive, to renew, to heal, to celebrate his creation. The Christian has not only the beauty of creation but also the glory of the resurrection to parade before the Lord. Worship is far more than asking God for help; it involves twisting God's arm with all his magnificent promises. When God appears ugly, remind him of the cross—nothing is more beautiful in his eyes.

Zophar's Defense of God's Wisdom (11)

Eliphaz interpreted Job's suffering as the corrective chastening of God (5:17). Bildad believed that penitent prayers and intercessory rites would erase the sins of Job's children which may have provoked Job's plight (8:4–5). Now Zophar argues that God in his mysterious sagacity has a salutary purpose for Job's tragedy which lies beyond his limited human vision to comprehend. Zophar interprets the mystery of God as a secret wisdom (v. 6), as an extremity of knowledge that lies beyond the boundaries of the created universe (vv. 7–8), and as a penetrating divine purpose which detects hidden human guilt (vv. 6, 10–11). Fools can never grasp such profound wisdom (v. 12). Job had found God's hidden purpose to be sardonic and ugly (10:13–14); Zophar declares it to be transcendent and sublime. His solution is similar to that of Bildad: submit to God's hidden purpose, confess your guilt, amend your sinful life, and stretch out your hands in penitent prayer to your

savior. Then life will again be blessed, prosperous and secure
(11:13–20).

There are times when preachers are tempted to expound or
counsel in the same vein as Zophar. The mystery of God is
simple answer to the problem of suffering; but it answers
nothing! The mental suffering of parishioners, the senseless
slaughter of a child in the street, bizarre atrocities, or natural
disasters in densely populated areas are readily chalked up to
the mystery of God. We assume God must have some hidden
purpose for allowing such misery on earth. For those in pain,
the mystery-of-God answer is a "cop out!" It explains nothing!
It offers no comfort, no empathy, no answer. It only rubs salt
into the wound. More salt is applied to Job's wound when
Zophar suggests a deep suppressed guilt which God in his wisdom plans to expose. He plays on the common fear of the sufferer that he or she must have done something evil to deserve
such trouble, but that God alone knows what it was.

A sermon entitled "When the Mystery of God Is Meaningless," would explore these themes anew. Such a topic would
enable an empathetic presentation of the pathos of Job, the
bitter screams of the oppressed and the cries of the man on
Calvary. An honest portrayal of these cries in the language of
Job will mean more for those in misery and mourning than all
the poetry of preachers about God's mysterious wisdom, all
the advice of Zophar about secret sins, and all the prattle of
Bildad about intercessary prayers. To confront God with our
human agony in all its ugliness is more meaningful than ca-
pitulating to the anonymous excuse of God's mystery. If the
great intercessors like Moses and Abraham can remind God of
his promises to provoke his saving intervention, we, like Job,
can expose our humanness, our suffering and our helplessness
to stir his sympathy. That approach is quite appropriate when
the mystery of God is meaningless (see also comments on
10:18–22).

Ask the Beasts (12:1–12)

It is typical of the wisdom tradition of the ancient Near
East that the world of nature provides models for human be-
havior and disguised clues to the hidden wisdom of the Creator in the universe (Prov 6:6; 30:18–33; 8:22–31). The elders
affirm this wisdom and hand down their knowledge of it from

generation to generation (12:12). Job sarcastically accuses his friends of claiming to have a corner on wisdom (v. 2). He, however, is just as intelligent and perceptive as they (v. 3). Yet they laugh him to scorn because he is an oddity, a human example of suffering who does not accept the classification to which they assign him. He is therefore a fool! A man in such obvious misery, they argue, must be suffering as a result of divine punishment being visited upon his wickedness. He fits the paradigm of the cursed wicked man (vv. 4–6). The wicked are cursed and the righteous are blessed. That is the logic of their theology. God does not arbitrarily afflict good human beings or shower the wicked with good fortunes.

"Ask the animals," replies Job, "they will teach you." This kind of arbitrary action is typical of the Almighty. A tree is struck by lightning, animals are drowned by floods, and birds die in forest fires through no fault of their own. They are the innocent victims of God's cosmic ways. Life and death are in God's hands and there is no apparent logic to the acts of destruction which befall nature. The animals are wise enough to know that Job's case is not unique. Ask the animals and they will confirm Job's argument.

If we are bold enough to preach on the relationship of human beings to their environment, then Job suggests that disruption and harmony in nature are not all caused by human greed. Violence may also be lurking in the structure of the cosmos itself. Violence, contends Job in the latter half of this chapter, is often the deliberate work of the Almighty. Talk to the animals and they will give you this sermon topic on "The Violence and Harmony of Nature." Observe their ways and they speak of God's wisdom. Listen to the Lord from his sermon on the mount and he will offer similar insights (Matt 6:25–34). Only in Christ is the hidden wisdom of God fully revealed (Col 1:15–2:5).

Hail to the King of Chaos (12:13–22)

This unit comprises the famous hymn of Job to the Lord of chaos and disorder. Previously Job had tackled the problem of God's power and exposed his violent acts of disturbance in the cosmic order (9:4–10). God's power was so great that Job was unable to force a trial and prove his integrity before heaven. God's power prevented justice from being executed rather

than guaranteeing it. Zophar had focused the question on
God's wisdom. God, he argues, operates on a higher plane
than insignificant humans like Job (11:7–11). Job replied that
the animals have sufficient understanding of God's ways to realize that disasters have no moral logic to them. They can be
quite arbitrary (12:1–12). If that is true, and if the way things
happen in the world is generally consistent with God's will,
argues Job, then we can deduce a portrait of God's wisdom
and might similar to that depicted in this classic hymn.

A sermon based on "The Hymn to the Lord of Chaos" could
be grounded in the sequence of the text.

(a) This God is the Lord of flood and famine; when he tears
down the heavens there is chaos and when he seals up
the skies there is drought (vv. 14–15). The Noah flood is
an example of his power, and the famine in Egypt typical of his wisdom.

(b) He is the power behind social and political disorder;
rulers are deposed, priests defrocked, and judges made
fools at his instigation (vv. 16–19).

(c) He is the master of folly; those who are expected to be
wise are deprived of their discernment and rendered
buffoons. This God has the characteristics of a trickster
(vv. 20, 24–25).

(d) He is the king of chaos; nations are broken at his command and the deep mysteries of the universe which he
reveals prove to be brazen acts of discord and disorder
(vv. 21–23).

Job's portrait derives from his compulsion to confront God
with the reality of evil in the world and the consequence of his
destructive actions as Lord of nature and society. In the last
analysis he is responsible; the fault is not entirely with
humans. From Job's position of powerlessness, God's deeds as
Lord of chaos seem to dominate. And he lets God know in no
uncertain terms!

Job's hymn acclaims God as the King of chaos and declares
his hidden wisdom the impulse for disorder. Psalm 104 celebrates God's wisdom (especially v. 24) as the source of a joy-
ous and orderly cosmos. The two hymns represent alternative
sides of reality in creation; both are worthy of reflection in
sermons on the wisdom and mystery of God (see the comments on chap. 11). His rule remains an enigma. Job exposes

the dark side; Psalm 104 acclaims its glory; Jesus reveals its meaning. In him the kingdom is a secret rule of a new order, a world of surprises greater than Job ever imagined (see Matt 13).

During the 1960's it was fashionable to experience multimedia happenings. Our senses were bombarded simultaneously with diverse noises, lights, images, and patterns of motion. Color slides would be projected continuously on, beside, around, and over each other. The effect was to be a total experience! For me the encounter gave the impression of chaos. I wanted to order and focus my viewing. On a much more profound level Job's experience leads us to consider a sermon on "Finding Order in Chaos."

(A) The Obvious God of Chaos

Job accuses God of being the King of Chaos. That seems to be the public image of God's rule. The world is in international chaos; rulers of nations rise and fall each year. Social and political chaos seems to reign in the big cities. Famine and oppression are rife. Racism and greed promote local chaos even in so-called free countries. Job was right!

The news media tend to relish highlighting the chaotic and cruel in the world so that we tend to accept violence as part of the very order of things. Where is God? That seems to be God's way of ruling, says Job in this chapter. Shaddai, the Almighty, is like the Hindu God Shiva, who not only dances the world into existence, but periodically dances its destruction.

(B) The Hidden God of Order

Amid a world of chaos each of us looks for a space we can order, a place where we are secure and comfortable; we construct a private world. But our space can be invaded and our world disrupted at any moment. Where has the God of peace, order and happiness been hiding? When we sense chaos we question God's rule. We respond like Job!

Nothing looked more like chaos than the week of Jesus' passion. Where was God then? Creating a new way, a deeper order of spiritual life! Jesus called it the King-

dom of God, an order of faith. Consider again his parable of the tares and the wheat (Matt 13:24–30).
Confusion seemed to prevail until the harvest.

The servant church is an underground order sown by
Christ in a world of chaos; its members share his peace.
For those scattered in a chaotic world the word of
Christ is a promise:

> "I have said this to you that you may have peace. In
> the world you will have tribulation; be of good cheer
> I have overcome the world" (John 16:33).

✓ Measuring our Mortality (14)

Unlike most of his previous speeches, Job's soliloquy on
the brevity of human life is not an argument directed against
his three friends. Here he explores the fragility and finality of
mortal existence as a common concern of human beings. If we
take Job's cue and preach on "The Measure of our Mortality"
we would highlight human life as

    (a) fleeting and fragile (vv. 1–3),

    (b) limited by destiny (vv. 5–6),

    (c) a one-time experience (vv. 7–12), and

    (d) pursued by the Lord of death (vv. 18–22).

A sermon on the measure of our mortality taken from this
passage in Job would need to take into account the OT
worldview within which the poet operates. For Job there is no
common belief in the resurrection; Sheol is the land of the
dead for all human beings. The grave is the end. Moreover, our
preaching from this text could include a balanced portrayal of
Job's anguish about mortality and Paul's message of rebirth
in Jesus Christ (1 Cor 15).

(a) Verses 1–3. Life is indeed a brief interlude on earth, an
interim liable to be fraught with excessive sorrows and misfortunes (see the comments on 1:20–21). Cancer can cut us
down in the prime of life. Man (*Adam* in the Hebrew) is born of
woman and therefore mortal, says Job. We are like the first
man Adam, says Paul, perishable creatures of dust (1 Cor
15:47–48).

(b) Verses 5–6. Not only is life short-lived, its limit is deter-
mined by God. Humans cannot extend their lives one minute
(see Matt 6:27). Their life span is fixed in the calendar of

destiny (see 3:3–6). Popular beliefs persist today that we cannot avoid premature death. "When your number is up, it's up!" is a common folk idea of determinism. For Paul, Jesus Christ died, not according to destiny, but according to the Scriptures (1 Cor 15:3). His death was part of a divine plan of salvation which renders calendars of destiny irrelevant. With his resurrection a new cosmic calendar is initiated; he is the first fruit of all who have fallen asleep (15:30).

(c) Verses 7–12. Job compares two forms of life, those of humans and trees. For trees there is always hope. If they are cut down they may experience life a second time and sprout forth anew. Not so human beings! Once they are laid low in the dust of the grave they do not rise again. They do not sprout new life and experience life a second time around. For Job there is no resurrection or reincarnation.

Paul speaks of two different bodily forms of existence—the terrestrial and the celestial (1 Cor 15:35–41). In the light of the resurrection of Jesus Christ, he announces two distinct forms of life for human beings—the perishable or physical and the imperishable or spiritual. While for Job humans are unable to rise from the dust, for Paul, they are sown like the seeds of a tree and rise to experience a new form of life. For the tree, hope means a repetition of physical life; for humans it means a life of a different order. They no longer bear the image of Adam, the man of dust, but of Christ the man of heaven. They now belong to a new realm of existence.

(d) Verses 18–22. For Job, life is lived over against God as the Lord of death and destruction. This God prevails over all powers. He reduces humans to dust and forces them to face their own death. They die in pain without hope or promise. They know only the sting of death and the power of God in death. Paul contends that death is now swallowed up in victory by the resurrection of Jesus Christ. Christ is now Lord over all powers; death is the last enemy to be destroyed. Christ, the Lord of life, renders death impotent. To God on high, Christ delivers the kingdom of life for all men to enjoy (1 Cor 15:24–28, 51–57).

The measure of our mortality depends on the yardstick we employ. In Adam we are reduced to dust; with Job we are welcomed to the womb of earth; in Christ we are translated to a new dimension. Yet all these realities reveal aspects of life as we experience it. The coming of Christ does not deny the truth of Job!

Peoples of all ages have speculated about life after death. Amid his exploration of life as transitory and tragic, Job too toys with the idea of a resurrection in vv. 13–17. A sermon based on these verses might be entitled "Stopover In Sheol." Job's argument and our reply might run as follows:

(A) In the face of our mortality, cries Job,
    (1) we have no hope of rejuvenation as plants (vv. 7–9);
    (2) we are destined to die and never rise (vv. 10–12);
    (3) we are no better than flowers that fade (vv. 1–2);
    (4) and there is no relief from suffering (vv. 5–6).
(B) Now God, suggests Job, what would you say to,
    (1) making Sheol a stopover, a temporary abode, safe from your anger (v. 13a);
    (2) and fixing a time when I could be resurrected (v. 13b);
    (3) I would wait patiently for your call (vv. 14–15);
    (4) and when I am raised you would seal my so-called sin in a bag and I would be vindicated (v. 17).
(C) But, Job, we reply, can that compare with
    (1) the stopover of Christ in Sheol where he conquered death by dying;
    (2) the resurrection of Christ which enables resurrection for all who live in him;
    (3) and the justification of sinners who believe in his death.

Job here looks for a resurrection from Sheol as a special individual privilege which would result in his being vindicated and declared innocent. For St. Paul, however, resurrection is a communal act for all who, though guilty, are united in Christ in whom they are justified.

Eliphaz on the Primal, Corrupt, and Wicked Human (15)

After a brief introduction in which he accuses Job of being a loud mouthed fool (vv. 1–6), Eliphaz makes three major points in response to Job. First he picks up the wisdom motif introduced by Zophar (see comments on chap. 11) and explored subsequently by Job (see comments on chap. 12). If Job claims a level of wisdom superior to the tested tradition of the elders, then he must be older than the elders. For Job to possess wisdom of a higher order than that of ordinary mortals he would need to have listened to the council of heaven at the time of creation and to have heard the deliberations of the Creator (vv. 7–13).

Eliphaz seems to be citing an old mythic tradition about a heavenly first man (Adam), who lived with God before creation and was privy to the planning of creation with Wisdom (see Prov 8:22–31, especially v. 30). By participating in the pre-creation council of God, the heavenly first man, born of God rather than woman, would know deeper mysteries of God's wisdom than humans born of woman and limited by mortality. The NT identifies a heavenly Adam with the person of Jesus Christ (1 Cor 15:47; Col 1:15). In his portrait of a primordial heavenly man Eliphaz anticipated, unknowingly, the preaching of St. Paul and the early church. In the strange economy of God, the critics of his ancient heros may be closer to the truth than they realize.

Job, of course, is not the primal wise man; he is a sinful mortal. Eliphaz' second point is to reiterate his prior assertion about the corruption of all human nature, Job's included. He intensifies his previous argument that human beings are impure by virtue of their position in the heirarchy of corruption (see comments on 4:17–19). Not only are humans naturally sinful but they also possess an insatiable thirst for evil. They live on wickedness as part of their normal fare (vv. 14–16).

Eliphaz spends the remainder of this chapter introducing the figure of the wicked human (vv. 17–35). The wicked are portrayed in elaborate detail. Such a theme is hardly popular today. Traditionally, lengthy portraits of the wicked served as moral deterrents for the faithful. The wisdom school identified the way of the wicked as a total life style and worldview opposed to the way of the righteous (Prov 4:14–18). If we take the sermon theme "What It's Like to be Wicked" the text of Eliphaz' speech would yield the following features:

(a) The wicked are consumed by an inner fear and a guilty conscience; like gangland killers they can expect a violent end at any time, a day of darkness that is prepared for them (vv. 20–24).

(b) They know their crimes are against God; eventually they will lose their ill-gotten gains and be swept away into the darkness (vv. 25–30).

(c) Yet they deceive themselves as they plan evil; they refuse to heed their fear that their reward will be emptiness and disaster (vv. 31–35).

Similar portraits of the wicked appear in the subsequent speeches of Bildad (18:5–21) and Zophar (20:4–29). To balance the image of the wicked offered by Eliphaz, the preacher could include the alternative picture painted by Job (see the comments on 21:7–30). Like Eliphaz, Paul has an interest in the fate of the wicked and frequently catalogues their sins (see Gal. 5:19–20).

The Search for Human Rights (16)

Here Job returns to the problem of a just trial which he introduced in chapter 9. He yearns for a court to convene and take up his case against God. The evidence against Job is overwhelming; God has seen to that! Job's pathetic appearance is itself a testimony to his guilt (vv. 6–8). God, in fact, is the guilty party. His sustained attacks on Job have left him subject to the insults and abuse of the wicked. He is an outcast (vv. 9–11). God has broken him asunder, dashed him in pieces, set him up as a target, slashed his kidneys, and poured out his gall. Job is a mutilated man (vv. 12–14). But Job is innocent. He has committed no violent crime. Instead of arrogance, he has exhibited humility. He has performed the appropriate rites of mourning and mortification, but to no avail (vv. 15–17).

God's crime against Job is so horrendous it will stir the earth to scream heavenward for vengeance (see Gen 4:10). The heavens will be forced to hear the voice of Job's blood crying for justice and bring the case to court (v. 13). Then a heavenly witness will testify to Job's innocence. Presumably this witness, like the umpire of 9:33, is a member of the heavenly court who is willing to espouse Job's cause (see Zech 3:1–5). The case is complicated by the fact that God, the guilty party, is also Job's accuser and ultimately his judge. Yet Job refuses to accept defeat. His witness would be his advocate before God, a true friend even when God is the enemy (see 6:14). The first line of verse 20 can be translated, "my interpreter, my friend." The friend's role is delineated in 6:14 (see the comments on 6:14–30). The interpreter has the task of mediating between conflicting parties (Gen 42:33; Job 33:23). Above all this figure would speak the truth and maintain the right of Job before God (vv. 20–21).

A sermon based on these concerns of Job could follow the model proposed for the text of 9:25–33. An alternative approach is suggested by the underlying demand of Job, his concern for "The Rights of a Man Before God." Human rights are of paramount concern in contemporary society. We endorse the right to free speech, to a good education, to humane treatment of our fellows, and so on. What are our human rights before God? Are we but pawns by virtue of our creation or mortality? Are we to be submissive victims of destiny? Have we no redress for the ills we suffer? Job, it seems, contends that as a human being he has certain rights. He asserts his right to a fair trial and an impartial judge. He ought to be able to count on God's justice. Without that right humans are at the whim of an arbitrary universe. He maintains that human beings have a right to be heard by God and not given the silent treatment. The right of communication is axiomatic for Job. Yet because of God's bias against Job he expects no genuine communication even if God does decide to speak (see 9:16–17). Elsewhere Job assumes the right to some divine mercy, even if it be but a momentary reprieve from suffering or the relief of the grave itself. After all, humans are the delicate handiwork of a gentle Creator. To be so formed is to expect loving providence from the Maker (see comments on 10:8–22). Job, however, contends that because of God's injustice all of his rights have been revoked. He has no standing before God.

A sermon on human rights before God would need to take into account the teaching of St. Paul that in terms of justification human beings have no rights before God. They have all violated God's law and come short of his glory (Rom 3). Salvation is not achieved by the deeds of man, but by faith in the person of Jesus Christ. Are Job and Paul in conflict? Or are the rights which Job is demanding valid even for us? Are they, in fact, endorsed by the person of Jesus Christ through whom God justifies the ungodly? And can these human rights be exercised with confidence through Christ our intercessor and mediator?

It has always seemed to me that the way people live their faith is either life-denying or life-affirming. Those who negate their humanity and consider it corrupt or illusory, attempt to deny, escape or shed their humanity by surrendering totally to God, the Absolute or another reality than their own. Those who affirm their humanity and its world as good, valuable or meaningful, seek to live their life to its fullest. They struggle against anything which would reduce that life in the slightest. They assert their rights as humans. Job belongs to this latter group and leads us to consider our "Human Rights Before God." He also invites us to compare his earlier cries in chapter 3.

(A) The Right to be Angry
    (1) To express our feelings of injustice and anger to God; to scream as Job! But anger without arrogance.
    (2) To take our frustrations out on God rather than on our family or ourselves—he is big enough to take it!
    (3) To let God know, as Job did, what it feels like to be the humans he has made us—creatures under pain and pressure (see Job 7).

(B) The Right to be Heard
    (1) When we have been treated unfairly by God, life or others.
    (2) When our faith is wavering and God seems distant.
    (3) When we are in need of hope, assurance and absolution; or when meaning in life fades (see 3:20–23).
    (4) To be heard but not to demand justification for our goodness; to assert our humanity before God without claiming to be God.

(C) The Right to an Interpreter
    (1) To find a mediator, like Job's, to interpret our needs before God and force him to listen (16:19–21).
    (2) To have a mediator before God the Judge, one who pleads for us in our guilt and weakness (see 19:25–26).
    (3) To know Christ as the interpreter of God, the one who revealed God and mediated salvation by foregoing his human rights.
    (4) To know Christ as Human when we express our anger, cry to be heard, and demand our rights.

Note: Job 17 reiterates several of the themes treated earlier, namely, Job's extreme anguish and his helpless situation in Sheol (see comments on 7:1–9; 14:7–12).

In chapter 18 Bildad expands on Eliphaz' portrait of the wicked man (see the comments on 15:17–35).

✓ The Search for a Redeemer (19)

In this chapter Job draws to a climax his search for someone who will promote his case with God. He longed for a mighty umpire who had the authority to force God into court and to mediate on Job's behalf (see comments on 9:32–35). He dreamed of a heavenly witness who would stand before the council on high and testify to his integrity when his innocent blood cried to heaven for vengeance (see comments on 16:18–22). Now he lifts his hope to an even higher level of expectation. He looks for a redeemer.

In the OT world, a redeemer (*goel*) was the person designated to maintain the continuity, unity, and integrity of a family. This figure would avenge the blood of a relative (Num 35:19), redeem members of the family sold into slavery (Lev 25:47–55), or protect a family line from extinction by marrying the widow of a relative (Deut 25:5–10). Boaz provides an ideal example of a redeemer; he assumes responsibility for Ruth and the property of her kinsman Elimelech (Ruth 4:1–6). Through the redeemer the family line can be protected from disaster or disgrace. Yahweh himself is often designated the Redeemer (*goel*) of Israel who delivers his people from annihilation (Exod 15:13).

Against this background a sermon on Job 19:25 could highlight "The Redeemer of Life." In outlining the theme of this text, the wider context of the chapter will be included so as to focus the depth of Job's search.

(a) *When Living is not Life* (vv. 2–10). Job's life is a living hell. He is tormented by insults from his friends, badgered by their insensitive counsel and bullied into confessing errors he has never committed (vv. 2–5). The real problem is God. By inflicting blatant curses on Job, God has marked him as guilty of insidious evils. At least that is the way others read his plight. His miserable condition is viewed as clear evidence of divine punishment provoked by Job's hidden guilt (v. 6; see the comments on 4:3–9). But Job claims he has committed no crime worthy of such ugly tragedies (see 16:17). His prayer is pure. Yet his cry of "Vengeance" against God goes unheeded by the heavens. His cry of "Murder" is lost; his blood is spilt in vain (see 16:18). God has ambushed him with a net, surrounded him with celestial troops and humiliated him with insulting attacks (vv. 7–12). Job, instead of being honored as a human being in the image of God, is stripped of his glory and honor (v. 8; cf Ps. 8 and comments on 7:11–21). Job is barely alive. Without hope (v. 10), without vindication (v. 6), and without honor (v. 9), there is no life, no *shalom*, no identity. If Job is to live, he needs a redeemer (see comments on chap. 16).

(b) *When Other Redeemers Fail* (vv. 13–20). Job's search for someone to stand beside him and take his case against God begins with his longing for a genuine friend.

A despairing man needs the loyalty of a friend
When he loses faith in the Almighty (6:14)

When one loses faith in the Almighty, one needs a human companion. When it is hard to trust God, one needs a fellow human being who will not be intimidated by the Almighty and desert. A friend is staunch even if it means taking sides against God (see comments on 2:11–13; 6:14–30).

Job has no such friend among his three companions (6:15–17). None of his friends, relatives or associates have the courage or compassion to stand by him in his hour of disgrace. He is an obnoxious embarrassment to all concerned (vv. 13–20). Job had longed for a friend (16:20) who would take up his case before the court of heaven. But all his expectations proved groundless. He has no friend, no redeemer, no mediator in heaven or on earth. They have all failed.

(c) *When the Great Redeemer Stands Forth* (vv. 23–27). The interpretation of these verses is notoriously difficult; they represent a particularly prickly cactus in the Joban textual garden. The position taken here is consistent with the translation of the Revised Standard Version which offers one legitimate option among many.

In spite of his accusations about the capricious character of his enemy (vv. 6–12), his total lack of support from his friends (vv. 13–22), and the apparent futility of his past search for a mediator, Job's faith reaches a new high. He has a final glorious vision of vindication. From the abyss of despair he beholds his integrity upheld. He is so firm in his conviction that he demands a permanent record of his testimony be inscribed in a book and engraved on stone (vv. 23–24). If all else fails he will have literary immortality (see 31:35–37).

He sees before him a redeemer, a figure who will rescue his

life from oblivion and his name from disgrace. In the background lies Job's relentless insistence on a court case in which he will "stand" before God acquitted. In the end, somewhere, somehow, the redeemer will "stand" forth in court to vindicate Job (v. 25). To "stand" in this context is a technical expression for appearing in court. Whether that "last" hour mentioned in Job's vision is a last minute reprieve when Job is almost dead, or whether it is a victorious justification after death is not clear. In either case Job's redeemer will force a confrontation with the Almighty and Job will see God (v. 26), something no man normally experiences (Ex 33:20). That radical experience will mean a new understanding and consciousness of God. And so it is for Job when he finally sees God from his bed of dust and ashes, sees God and survives, sees God and lives (42:5–6).

The magnificence of Job's vision lies in his hope of a redeemer who is greater than any previous OT heroes. He anticipated a new kind of friend from above, a mysterious redeemer who would not be daunted by God's anger, a mediator like Moses who brought his people to "see God" (Ex 24:9–11; 32:7–14). Job's redeemer is a forerunner of Jesus Christ. He lives to redeem life, to enable human beings to experience the presence of God—to see God! Through this redeemer God confirms human identity as valuable and human life as meaningful.

There is nothing in this text about the resurrection of the redeemer, in spite of the rendering in Handel's *Messiah*. The focus is on the life-giving role of the redeemer; he rescues his friends from oblivion. He interprets their case to God and renews their lives in the face of death. In NT terms, those in Christ are a new creation, new beings with new identities. Their integrity has been found in Jesus Christ (2 Cor. 5:16–21). In him they become "the righteousness of God."

Some years ago I returned to the old bluestone farmhouse of my pioneer great grandfather in Australia. Alas, the house was inhabited by sheep and pigeons. If only, I thought, someone had redeemed that homestead while it was still habitable. We did, however, redeem the memory of my great grandfather and great grandmother by erecting a plaque to honor their lives. As our lives spin away many of us begin "Dreaming Of A Redeemer."

(A) Dreaming of Our Redeemers
  (1) We look for someone to redeem our lives, hopes, names, value from oblivion just as the redeemer in Israel redeemed the family line, name or property.
  (2) Gurus and great religious leaders rise as modern day redeemers—at least they promise to redeem our lives from oblivion or meaninglessness.
  (3) Politicians and radicals promise to redeem our life, land and liberty.
(B) Job's Dreaming
  (1) Job sought someone, a heavenly interpreter (see 9:32–34), a celestial witness (16:19–21), and a redeemer (19:25–26) who would rise on his behalf.
  (2) Job wanted someone to redeem his integrity and prove him innocent, the victim of injustice at the hands of God.
  (3) But Job found no one to stand up, even on the dust of his grave, to redeem him; he faced God alone.
(C) More Than a Dreamer
  (1) Jesus Christ comes as more than a dream, a dreamer, a fulfilled hope—he comes in human form.
  (2) He refuses to be a political, national or short-term redeemer of people; he is more than Job dreamed.
  (3) He comes to redeem from death, final death; he thereby redeems us by his own death to have a life, name and value in him that is eternal; he gave his life a ransom (Mark 10:45).

Note: Zophar's speech in chapter 20 is a lengthy portrait of the ways and fate of the wicked tyrant. For a similar description of the wicked man see the comments on 15:20–35.

Why Do the Wicked Prosper? (21)

The correlative of Job's contention that the innocent suffer unjustly is the contention that the wicked prosper *gratis*. Eliphaz, Bildad, and Zophar had each offered expansive portraits of the wicked (15:17–35; 18:15–21; 20:4–29). In connection with Eliphaz' description we proposed a sermon on "What It's Like to be Wicked." A corresponding sermon with the same title based on Job's assertions in this chapter would produce a radically different outline.

(a) The wicked enjoy power and prosperity. Their children are healthy, their flocks are fertile, their lives full of celebration and their death peaceful (vv. 7–13).

(b) The wicked can flaunt the Almighty and survive. They can ignore his ways and prosper without turning to him for aid (vv. 14–15).

(c) The wicked escape God's judgment. Where is the justice, cries Job, in deferring God's wrath and visiting his punishment on the children (vv. 17–21).

(d) The wicked die after enjoying a full life while the righteous experience bitterness of soul (vv. 23–26).

(e) The wicked tyrant enjoys the greatest good. He escapes disasters; he is too powerful to be confronted with his evil deeds and travels to his grave with a grand display of splendor. Ask any traveller abroad (vv. 27–33)!

Job finds no comfort in the splendid images of the wicked proffered by his friends. Such pictures offer no solace. They only intensify the pain in Job's soul. God's justice appears to be so arbitrary; he himself seems to attack and persecute the innocent (see Jer 12:1–4). It is typical of the lament Psalms that God is summoned to execute vengeance on the wicked who persecute the faithful. By so doing God identifies with the faithful and demonstrates his righteousness (see Pss 17; 22; 69).

Job's portrait of the wicked nullifies those of his friends who are already to classify Job in the same category. Job has one overriding concern—the vindication of his own righteousness before God. The traditional law of retribution in Deuteronomy stated that the wicked would be cursed and the righteous blessed (see Deut 28). Job finds that this law does not operate in his life. When his friends argue the reverse of that law and contend that a suffering creature like Job must have been cursed because of some evil deed, he knows their interpretation of that law is invalid (see comment on 4:3–9). His knowledge and description of the prosperous wicked makes that kind of reverse interpretation of the law ludicrous.

Yet the portraits of Eliphaz and Job stand side by side in the biblical text. They appear to be diametrically opposed images. Yet both are, to some extent, living reflections of the ambiguity of reality. A related ambiguous scene is depicted in the NT when the judge calls all to account for their deeds. The rewards and punishments meted out to the nations of the earth are based on deeds of kindness to the King which the people did not even realize they were performing or neglecting to perform (Matt 25:31–46).

Recently I saw a man in his car chase a man on foot and attempt to kill him with the car. It was as though I were watching a violent crime movie. The anger of the driver and the dread of the victim surrounded me. The car crashed after hitting the victim and injuring innocent bystanders. Those who watched remained passive, numb and uninvolved. I wondered again about the topic, "Why Do the Wicked Prosper?" Why Job?

    (a) Because we are too apathetic? we see the evil as too vast and leave its solution to the politicians?

    (b) Because we identify the wrong people as the wicked? we punish the petty criminals while the serious wicked prosper?

    (c) Because we have accepted wickedness and violence as an inevitable part of our modern world—and lock our doors?

    (d) Because corruption runs deeper than one attempted kill-and-run; it threatens us and makes us impotent?

    (e) Because God likes it to happen, as Job suggests, or because he has another purpose? If so, what is it?

We can, of course, point to the judgment day, when justice of a higher order will be administered (Matt 25:31–46). We can look again to the cross where God's Son suffered unjustly at the hands of the wicked who prospered that day. And we can affirm that Christ came to win the ultimate victory over death and evil. But for now, with Job, we protest the prosperity of the wicked at the expense of the innocent. And we look for those who suffer with Christ and Job to become agents of justice in the earth.

Note: In his final speech (chap. 22) Eliphaz publicly accuses Job of being a wicked man (v. 5). God's judgment against him is therefore clear evidence of divine justice.

In chapter 23, Job reiterates his desire for a court case with God, in spite of God's biased stance. The theme is discussed in connection with 9:1–24; 9:25–35; 16 and 19.

Entering the World of the Poor (24:5–12)

We construct our world from the realities we face or find. Each world, whether it be that of the businesswoman or the priest, has a symbol system for meaning and survival. For most people the world of the poor, the rag pickers and bag ladies of the inner city, the street orphans of the slums, or the homeless vagrants of the ghetto, is virtually impossible to comprehend. Yet it was a mark of true justice in the ancient Near East when a leader espoused the cause of the poor, the widow, and the orphan. In this text, the writer takes us beyond justice to empathy. We enter vicariously into the world of the poor; our attitude is to be one of genuine compassion rather than blind paternalism. In that line hides a sermon: "Passion or Paternalism for the Poor?"

Job 24 is an anonymous discourse with no introduction. Vv. 5–12 focus on the plight of the poor; the remaining verses deal with the ways of the wicked and their anticipated downfall in terms similar to those outlined by the friends (see 15:17–35; 18:5–21; 20:4–29).

What is it like to live in the world of the poor? To be poor means to know injustice, to be thrust off the road as useless rubbish. Finding food involves scouring the streets or the fields for a discarded morsel. Cold penetrates one's very soul and bitter weather one's inner being. Hunger is a way of life, bare subsistence a life style, and death a constant companion. The poor live with the dying, the diseased, and the destitute. They know the raw side of life, a world of incquity and inequality. Job understands—with a passion! No paternalistic tokens of charity will change their world. The rejected poor and the fugitive Job are brothers in despair. The integrity of the oppressed and suffering soul is their common cry. To uphold that cry is justice! To promote such justice is the demand laid on the listener by this text. The demand is reiterated by James (1:26–2:7).

Note: Bildad's portrait of the corruption of humans (25:2–6) is a variation of Eliphaz' argument in 4:17–19 and is discussed at that point. In my opinion 26:5–14 is a continuation of Bildad's speech in chapter 25. His speech exalts the power and wisdom of God's cosmic design much as the anonymous writer does in chapter 28 and the poet in 38–39. Chapter 27 seems to be composed of a brief speech by Job (vv. 1–7) in which Job reasserts his innocence (see the comments on 16:15–22 and chap. 31) and an anonymous discourse about the fate of the wicked (vv. 8–23; see comments on 15:17–35).

A Series of Answers:
More Riddles
(Job 28–42)

The Bible has the answer! That is the common belief of many Christians. No matter what the question, the answer can be found in the Bible. Somewhere in its pages God has spoken and his answer to the conundrums of life can be found. If a preacher is worth his salt, he will distil the Bible into a set of easy answers for the average Christian.

The book of Job challenges this approach. The long series of arguments and accusations by Job against God and his three friends leave us with a mountain of unanswered questions. Job, too, demands an answer, a trial to vindicate his integrity. Through the previous cycle of speeches we have struggled with Job and his friends to understand the nature and meaning of suffering. What's it all about? Why innocent suffering? Why iniquity rampant in the world? The questions posed are endless and eternal.

Finally the time comes for answers, for summation and a verdict in the great debate. But instead of discovering clear and simple answers we find a series of climaxes that pose new riddles. Just as Jesus often answered his gainsayers with questions which set their problems into a whole new context (Matt 9:5; Mark 11:30), so the book of Job concludes with one finale after another, each raising new provocative questions.

Job's closing speech recounts his past life of virtue, his present state of misery, and his public vow of innocence (chaps. 29–31). He leaves us wondering "Can anyone be that good?" He forces God's arm by swearing an oath. He leaves us asking whether we have the right to tackle God in a similar manner and demand divine action to resolve our crises. May we make similar oaths with curses implied? When Elihu intrudes after the great debate is concluded, his answer seems an anticlimax. This angry youth steps out of the shadows and claims to know all the answers, intuitively (chaps. 32–37). Yet what he is and what he says remain an enigma. Or are his youthful out-

bursts somehow closer to the truth than all the deliberations
of his wise elders?

The grand finale is the word of Yahweh from the whirlwind. He, in all his majestic power, responds to thirty six
chapters of debate and searching with an impressive array of
cosmic questions. His reponse is an avalanche of complex riddles, his word a magical mystery tour of the primordial universe. He forces the searching Job to search again (chaps. 38–
41). Job returns to the beginning, to the dust of his humanity
(42:1–6).

The story appended to these poetic climaxes provides us
with a happy ending, but an awkward one (42:7–17). It makes
the book into an ancient comedy; after all, things do not turn
out that way in real life! The portrait of Job's suffering may
have been larger than life, but his subsequent blessings are
too good to be true. Job is both a saint and a rebel. We struggle
with him in his combat with the Almighty. We empathize
with his passion and humanity. In the end, however, he leaves
us searching his search for meaning in our own lives.

The Eternal Quest for Wisdom (28)

Gurus, mystics, and pop psychologists offer the world a
path to discover hidden wisdom. Their tantalizing books are
paraded in streets, stores, and temples. Human beings are
lured by the promise of a deeper knowledge that will give
them power, peace, and meaning in life. Dissatisfaction with
contemporary life and the inherent desire of humans to discover new truths perpetuate "The Eternal Quest For Wisdom," a sermon topic as timely today as in the day of Job.

This poem on the quest for wisdom is an independent discourse which seems to have no direct connection with the arguments of Job or his three friends. Though wisdom is a
concern of the friends (8:8–10; 11:6–11; 15:7–8), Job's image
of the wisdom of God as a twisted pattern of deceit and disorder is at odds with the theology of this poem (see comments on
12:13–25).

The Eternal Quest for Wisdom described in this lyrical text
can be appreciated in several ways.

(a) *It is an impulse for bold exploration* (vv. 1–11). The min-
ing exploits of Solomon and his latter day counterparts have
led human beings to penetrate the depths of the earth to find

gold, metal ore, and precious stones. They have located that hidden core of the earth where, by some mysterious subterranean fire, rock is changed into valuable metal (vv. 5–6). Even the sharp eye of the falcon overhead cannot catch a glimpse of this mystery happening beneath the earth's surface (v. 7). Human beings begin to match the power and wisdom of the gods when they overthrow mountains or dam up rivers (vv. 9–10).

Is any feat beyond human skill, asks the poet? Is there any limit to human knowledge? From the depths of space to the deep of the brain the search for knowledge continues. The quest is familiar to each of us.

(b) *It provokes a search for Wisdom herself* (vv. 12–22). Not satisfied with a wealth of knowledge about the world, humans seek the principle or power behind this knowledge and hope to control it. Wisdom is portrayed here as a silent force operating behind the scenes in the cosmos. The question is whether she can be located? Is there a center where wisdom is concentrated or a home where she resides?

In Proverbs, Wisdom invites any searcher to enter her abode and learn her hidden truths (4:7–12; 9:1–6). Here the message is different. In the last analysis wisdom is inaccessible, her abode beyond the exploration potential of humans (vv. 20–21). The very "deeps" of the cosmos do not know her home (v. 14); she existed before they were even created (Prov 8:24). The realms of death have heard of her only by rumor (v. 22). Wisdom is a commodity of a different order than ordinary skills or property. No treasure trove of precious goods could buy or bribe Lady Wisdom (vv. 15–19).

(c) *It leads to the Lord of Wisdom* (vv. 23–27). The human quest for wisdom leads eventually to the Lord who knows Wisdom and her ways. Her hidden abode and its secret access are known to the Almighty. Wisdom is here portrayed as a feminine power somewhat independent of God. She is more than an attribute of the divine Ruler. In Prov 8:22–31, she is the ingenious counsellor or artisan who guides Yahweh in ordering the cosmos and the playful companion who celebrates the creation event with him. There is more to Wisdom than the superior skill of God. She is the intangible spirit of the universe which he once discovered for himself (v. 27). Beyond all cosmic limits, all the fixed patterns for the forces of heaven and earth, beyond, behind, and within the creation itself he discovered a mystery in his own work. That mystery is Wisdom! We know her through him; we find a rumor of her by walking the pathways of creation with him. Is that the final experience of Job in chapters 38–39? The author of this poem seems to suggest so!

The portrait of Wisdom as elusive and inaccessible prompted a more traditional postscript in the vein of later wisdom theologians (v. 28). The fear and worship of Yahweh, they proclaimed, will lead to wisdom and a life of righteousness will yield true sagacity (Prov 1:2–7). But for the poet of Job 28, wisdom is an elusive principle and the path to her abode a tantalizing mystery. She is hidden in Jesus Christ, adds Paul centuries later (Col 2:3).

An Oath, a Lifetime and a Final Word (31)

Job 29–31 is a summation of Job's case before the high court of the Almighty. He surveys those better days when his counsel was revered and his name synonymous with justice and compassion (chap. 29). He recapitulates the humiliation of his recent experiences; he is a now a man abused by the dregs of society (30:1–15) and reduced by a cruel God to ignominy and despair (30:16–23). He has no mediator, no redeemer, no friend but the jackals (30:24–31).

Job's summation goes beyond a regurgitation of his past arguments and agonies. He is now ready to answer all the accusations and inuendoes about his guilt with a bold oath of innocence. He confronts God directly with his vow. If he were lying his oath would incur an automatic divine curse. Job, however, is certain of his innocence. The catalogue of vices he includes in his oath represent a wide ranges of social, moral, political, and private wrongs (31:1–34). Job contends that he is guilty of no injustice; his life has been a paragon of integrity. If he were lying God would be forced to impose the appropriate curse. There is the point of Job's final word. The corresponding sermon theme is "When the Time Comes to Force God's Hand."

For Job the negotiations were over, the time for pleading was past, the disputations about God's justice and wisdom had been concluded, and the anticipated redeemer had not come to rescue Job before the bar of justice. The deadline had been reached! Job's wife had suggested forcing God's hand by a direct curse on God. "Do you still hold to your integrity? Curse God and die (2:9)." Her advice would have ended Job's plight swiftly. Job, however, did hold to his integrity. In fact, he now uses that very integrity as the basis for his oath. His integrity becomes the vehicle for forcing God to pronounce the curse should Job's oath prove false.

Job's final word functions as an ultimatum. He throws down the gauntlet before his God. "Here is my signature! Let the Almighty answer me" (v. 35). He has signed his oath with his suffering. He is ready for the attendant curse should he be lying. He demands a corresponding document from God, his accuser (see 19:23–24). If there were such a script Job is sure it would necessarily declare his innocence and he could wear it proudly (vv. 36–37). (Note that the *RSV* rendering "indictment" in verse 35 is literally a "written script" in the Hebrew; it can be either an indictment or an acquittal depending on the context.)

Job has reached the breaking point, the point where prayers and screams are useless. He has spent his anger and taken action. He has stated his case and declared his oath. Job will now be silent. It is up to God the Almighty to break that silence with a word, be it curse or blessing. How often do we come to such an awesome moment when we force the hand of God? Or is it for Christians forcing the hand of Christ? (see the comments on chap. 16).

Comparable decisive moments occur in the lives of Abraham, Moses, and Jesus. Bargaining for the lives of those in Sodom, Abraham forces God to accept a lower quota of righteous in the city (Gen 18:22–33). When the children of Israel murmur about the lack of meat in their manna diet God's anger blazes down upon them. Moses, however, is ready to die rather than live with such anger. "Kill me at once," he cries, "that I may not see my wretchedness" (Num 11:15). For Jesus that moment came in the Garden of Gethsemane...and for God himself when his Son was on the cross.

Perodically each of us likes to play, to look for the whimsical in the world. There is very little humor, frolic or serendipity in Job. His cries are deadly serious. Yet the close of Job's final speech has a touch of humor, ironic though it may be. In line with this, I suggest a topic like "The Little Prince," or "No

Time for Gnomes," and a sermon could explore the following progression.

    (a) Job claims to be innocent of any crime worthy of his suffering.

    (b) He is willing to force God's hand by declaring an oath that would kill or clear Job (27:1–6).

    (c) He has been deserted by all his friends; the jackals alone are his brothers now (30:29).

    (d) He challenges God to write his indictment on a scroll with the charges against him (31:35).

    (e) If God complies Job will wear the scroll as a crown and march boldly as a prince before a Judge (31:36–37). How ludicrous and comical! This emaciated man, covered with boils and ashes, sees himself rising from his heap and marching proudly before the judge wearing, of all things a "paper" crown.

    (f) Job's integrity, however, lies within him, not in his crown. Compare the crown of thorns, the mocked king of the Jews, and the royal robe worn by Jesus the fisherman.

Clearly this was no time for gnomes in Job's life or Jesus' passion. It was a time when the ludicrous was profound and when mockery had enduring meaning. But when the ordeal is over Job celebrated life with three beautiful daughters just as Jesus looked forward to eating and drinking with his followers in the Kingdom.

Elihu, the Enigmatic Boy (33)

Elihu is an enigmatic figure, a brash theologian, a clever young fool. Into the stillness of the awesome moment that follows Job's final word flung in the face of God, Elihu intrudes like a thundering elephant. He explodes with sudden passion against Job and his three friends for the folly of their discourse. He invades God's space, anticipates portions of God's speech and delays God's word from the whirlwind (32:1–3). He is ready to defend God at all costs and cut Job down to size. He admits he is rather young and asserts that he has only remained silent out of deference to the age of his companions. Finally he explodes with righteous anger (32:4–7).

In spite of his age Elihu claims wisdom. That wisdom, he contends, is imparted directly from the spirit of the Almighty.

Inspiration is inherent in all human beings; it is part of their creation (32:8–10; 33:3–4). His claim to authority is grounded in his human nature. The boy was born wise! In the interest of bringing the communication gap between the generations a sermon on "The Wisdom of Inspired Youth" has appeal. Features of this sermon grounded in Job 33 could create the following pattern.

(a) *I Am Human, Like You* (vv. 3–7). The boy Elihu has a right to be heard. What he says is just as sincere as all the discourses of the elders. His thoughts come direct from the heart, without equivocation or camouflage (v. 3). He is filled with the same divine life-giving spirit that creates intelligence and insight in all humans (v. 4). He is an ordinary mortal made of clay. There is no need for his elders to be afraid of him (vv. 6–7). Who can gainsay his argument? Are the thoughts of youth usually suppressed in the community of faith? Does youth necessarily lack wisdom? Is the boy Jesus in the temple the only exception (Luke 2:41–51)?

(b) *I Can Hear You* (vv. 8–14). Elihu has been silent for a long time. Unlike others who only hear what they want to hear, Elihu knows precisely what Job is saying. "Job is innocent; his enemy is guilty!" Elihu is right. That was Job's contention in a nutshell. Elihu's verdict is just as succinct and to the point. "Job, you're wrong! God is bigger than you. You should know better than to take him to court" (vv. 8–13). It is often the child who cuts through the verbiage to discern the heart of the matter. From the mouth of babes the hard word is often spoken more honestly.

(c) *And I Can Hear God* (vv. 15–22). The child who speaks with God in the night may often be closer to the truth than all the professional diviners attempting to read the signs of God's will in the world. God speaks to humans even if they do not always hear him, contends Elihu. Apparently Elihu has himself experienced the voice of God (v. 14). Dreams are one source of divine messages. If you listen to your nightmares, suggests Elihu, they will keep you humble and rescue you from the grave (vv. 15–18). If you accept your sufferings as disciplinary warnings they will lead you to repentance and salvation from the underworld (vv. 19–22; see comments on 5:17–27).

(d) *But God Hears Our Interpreter* (vv. 23–30). Elihu, like many children, has no problem with an angel intervening on behalf of a human being. Such a mediator, or more precisely interpreter, translates our human needs into God's language (see comments on chap. 16). He pleads for mercy and offers a ransom for the life of the human being involved (see Ex 30:12). The response of the suffering individual is one of grateful repentance. The sufferer makes confession and accepts the gift of new life from the Creator. The interpreter wins God's favor with a ransom and the penitent sufferer is restored to health.

Admittedly this was not Job's idea of a redeemer. He searched for a celestial friend who would vindicate his innocence and prove God wrong (see comments on Job 19). Yet in the bold wisdom of this youth a model for reconciliation is proposed which anticipates the NT concept of Jesus Christ the mediator who freely offers his life a ransom to redeem the lives of those who trust in him. Such is the wisdom of inspired youth. Is that wisdom far from the child faith that marks entry into the Kingdom of Heaven?

I have always been bothered when people speak of having a simple faith or assert that faith is simple. I also have the hunch that the poet of Job placed the speech of Elihu here as a deliberate contrast to the profound statement about the inscrutability of God's wisdom in chap. 28. Job has just experienced deep agony of soul; Elihu, the impetuous twit, claims intuitively to know the answers to Job's problems. Indeed, we ought to ask Elihu, "Is There Such a Thing as Simple Faith?"

(A) The Trend to Be Simplistic
    (1) Knowledge in our contemporary world tends to be reduced to tabloid answers and easy solutions—e.g., "I'm O.K. You're O.K."
    (2) The Christian life is often reduced to "All you need is Love."
    (3) The Christian faith is reduced to "simple faith without all that theology," or "just believe in Jesus!"
    (4) Elihu answers in simple black and white: "Job, you are wrong" (33:2).

(B) The Claim to Direct Knowledge
    (1) Serious probing of God's mysterious ways is often considered dangerous.
    (2) Like Elihu, many of us want to claim a direct line

with God; having his spirit we know all truth, we know his will!

(3) Like Elihu, we look for easy answers, immediate answers and not the struggle or turmoil of Job.

(4) But for Job, and us, the answer lies in the struggle.

(C) The Faith Is Not Simple

(1) Job's deep faith and understanding was won in his long conflict with God (see chap. 10 and 42:1–6).

(2) The God we know through Job is a complex being; at times he appears alien (see 12:13–25), insidious (chap. 7) or cruel (6:4). Yet Job spoke "right" of God (42:7–8)!

(3) The Christ we know from the Gospels is no simple fisherman performing miracles; he speaks in parables, offers a new rule and promises life through his death. That's complex!

(4) Even on the night of his betrayal Jesus' disciples did not understand the depth of it all (see Luke 22:38); there always was a secret at work (Mark 8:31–33); even after the resurrection some disciples doubted (Matt 28:17).

Note: Since the remaining chapters of Elihu (34–37) reiterate many of the arguments of the three friends and anticipate several of Yahweh's speeches from the whirlwind no comment is made on them here.

The Whisper from the Whirlwind (38:1–3)

The grand theophanies of Yahweh assume many forms in the OT. From the burning bush to the fiery cloud on Sinai (Ex 24), from the thundering voice of the storm (Ps 29) to the still small voice from the cave (1 Kings 19), he communicates his presence. Deep in a tempest that blows across his ash-heap Job hears a voice, a whisper from the whirlwind. The voice does not bother to answer the precise questions Job had asked, nor does it summon Job to court as Job had commanded. The Almighty had been roused from his celestial abode by the persistent challenge of a human being. His cosmic rest had been disturbed. "Who on Earth Is This Man?" is God's natural response and a natural theme for a sermon.

Job is now issued a new challenge. Many of his speeches questioned God's eternal counsel, the divine blueprint for managing the universe and ordering the cosmos (Isa 46:10). Before he answers Job there are a few questions God would like to ask. Fair enough! Job is not reduced to a crumbling heap. He is honored by a direct confrontation, a personal interview with the Almighty; he is challenged to be a man and answer heaven. Who on earth is this man?

"Where were you when I laid the foundations of the earth?. . . Surely you know!" asks God (vv. 4–5). What kind of question is that? Is God merely being sarcastic. After all Job was not around when creation got under way. Unless God has someone else in mind, someone like the heavenly First Man mentioned by Eliphaz (see the comments on chap. 15). Is God addressing Job as if he were a celestial Adam who accompanied the Creator when he established the universe just as Wisdom had done (Prov 8:22–31)? Who on earth is this man that God should treat him as a creation companion?

"Where is the way to the dwelling of light. . .? You know, for you were born then, and the number of your days is great" (vv. 19–21). Is the sarcasm intensifying or is God, in fact, forcing Job to assume the role of the first born man? If Job is this heavenly First Man then he is as old as creation, aware of the whole creation process and the entire course of history. He would then have the wisdom to answer the Almighty. Who on earth is this man, as old as the hills themselves?

Job had forced the hand of God (see comments on chap. 31). He had presumed to take on God, as Jacob of old had done (Gen 32:22–32). Job's challenge is met with a comparable parry from above, a whisper from the whirlwind demanding the identity of this man. Is this the patient Job, a fool obscuring the design of creation, the first born man in creation or a heavenly human full of wisdom?

In that question, the multiple identity of each human being before God is drawn into focus. The personal and rhetorical questions posed by Yahweh force humans to seek more than a meek self-image in their identity. They are Eve and Adam, wise and foolish, complex and simple, child and parent, intruders in God's universe and companions in his creation. Who on earth are they? Who on earth are we? (see also the comments on 40:6–14).

The Web of Creation (38:4– 39:30)

It is difficult to capture in commentary the majestic and musical patterns of creation depicted in Job 38– 39. The intricate interplay of creative deeds and cosmic structures is cited as evidence of God's wise plan for the world. The operating universe is a web of wisdom. A sermon on "Creation As The Web Of Wisdom" could draw together many of the poetic and mythic strands in these chapters. The following patterns of wisdom are but a few worthy of exploration.

(a) *The Dimensions of the Deep.* The Creator is portrayed as a master architect, establishing the foundations of the earth at the bottom of the watery deeps (vv. 4– 6; see Prov 3:19). These cosmic pillars give stability to the universe (see Ps 93:1– 5). Where the waters of the deep burst forth to the surface like a child, God has provided a suitable place for them to play. These waters are the sea, cradled in clouds like a child, set down in its play pen and ordered never to cross the shoreline or flood the earth (vv. 8– 11). Below the surface the deeps are structured as subterranean springs, the abode of the dead and the land of darkness (vv. 16– 17). The earth, with all its hidden dimensions below the surface, is a challenge to the wisdom of humans (v. 18; see comments on chap. 28).

(b) *The Highways of Heaven.* Crisscrossing the heavens are pathways to the appointed homes of the celestial powers. Light has its own dwelling and darkness its abode (vv. 19– 20). Snow and hail are appropriately housed. A place is assigned for lightning (RSV "light") and wind to be dispensed upon the earth (vv. 22– 24). The rain and the thunderbolt do not fall at random; they have designated paths to follow (vv. 25– 27). The constellations, likewise, are appointed their positions in the zodiac and the patterns of the heavens are meticulously maintained by the power of God's wisdom (vv. 31– 37). Who would dare challenge this cosmic design and pronounce it arbitrary? Yet such was Job's charge (see comments on 12:13– 22).

(c) *The Splendor of the Animals.* The animal world is a magnificent testimony to God's providence and wisdom. The lions know how to find prey for their young (vv. 39– 40). Instinctively the mountain goats follow their appointed mating seasons (39:1– 4). It is natural for the wild ass and the wild ox to relish the open steppes; they do not belong with domesticated beasts in the economy of creation (vv. 5–12). The horse is a symbol of glorious animal power, a beast exulting in the frenzy of battle (vv. 19–25). The hawk and the eagle have an inner wisdom that enables them to soar to great heights and survive (vv. 26 – 30).

For those few creatures, like the ostrich, which seem to lack innate wisdom, God intervenes directly to protect their young (vv. 13–18). The laws of nature evident in the world of the animals testify to the wise providence of the Almighty. Why should man be different, Job, and ask for superior knowledge? Why should humans yearn for the tree of knowing good and evil?

(d) *The Celebration of Creation.* The Creator rejoices in his creation. A sense of his pride and delight are conveyed through the lyrical language of these chapters. The morning stars sang and the sons of God rejoiced when creation began (38:7). The celestial powers still celebrate with the Creator in his continuing creation, just as wisdom once did (Prov 8:30–31). The prayer of the Psalmist still rings true, "May the glory of the Lord endure forever, may the Lord rejoice in his creative work" (Ps 104:31). The same glory appeared at Bethlehem and the celebration of the heavens broke through for humans to hear. "Glory to God in the highest!"

A friend of mine once lived on the other side of the tracks. He would walk those barren tracks to school all through the winter. With the first dandelion, a spot of yellow in the soot, he knew it was Spring. He ran home celebrating, holding the flower in his hand. In the face of creation's majesty why do we turn to simple symbols for our celebration? In the light of Job 38 and 39, "Who Needs Dandelions?" We do.

(A) Because we cannot comprehend the cosmos the total cosmos any more than Job could!

    (1) God challenges Job to answer his enigmas about the way the world was constructed. We, like Job, are non-plussed!

    (2) God challenges Job to recall the celebration of the morning stars when the world was created. We, like Job, cannot return to that primal era.

    (3) God challenges us to interpret the galaxies above us, the geological system beneath us and the neuro-

system within us. But we remain amazed. We cannot grasp the immensity of the cosmos.

(B) Because we need a focal point for celebrating life within the cosmos!

    (1) Surprise pieces, like dandelions, give us a focus for celebrating God's whole world.

    (2) We can celebrate the resurrection, not in the emergence of new galaxies, but in the simple act of Jesus breaking bread with his disciples.

    (3) We understand the providence of God in the universe when we know his healing in our own lives.

We celebrate the grandeur of the cosmos when we find it reflected in the face of the dandelion shining in the dust—and we are surprised by the grandeur of God's world, in our own back yard!

Would You Like to Be Superman? (40:6–14)

"Who on earth is this man?" whispered the Almighty from the whirlwind (see comments on 38:1–3). Now he changes his tone and thunders a challenge. Would you like to be my equal? Would you like to match my power and put me in the wrong so that you can be vindicated? Well, if you want to play superman, this is your agenda.

(a) *First, a Spectacular Entry* (v. 10). Job is to array himself with the splendor of the divine ruler and display his royal glory to the world. Nothing short of a theophany is demanded.

(b) *Next, a Demonstration of Justice* (vv. 11–12). Job is to unleash his thunderbolts, punish the wicked and send them into oblivion. He is to be unequivocal in his humiliation of the ungodly.

(c) *Finally, a Battle with Chaos* (40:15–41:34). Job is confronted with two monsters of mythology, Behemoth and Leviathan (40:15; 41:1). They symbolize those forces which threaten to overwhelm creation at any time. They are part of the complex cosmos whose hidden powers Job will need to keep in balance.

(d) *Then I Will Accept You as Victor* (40:14). If Job can control chaos, administer uniform justice, and rule the world by the power of his own might, God will concede defeat. Job can win his own case. Job, however, needs to put himself in God's shoes before he will ever appreciate the complexity of cosmic wisdom, the delicate balance of positive and negative forces at work in the universe. It is one thing to be superman or superwoman in the popular sense, to defy the laws of nature and fight crime on a simplistic level. It is quite a different story being God. The interplay of chaos and order, of death and life, of destruction and creation, is far more difficult to manage than any computer mind or super brain. The moment Job is challenged he knows his limitations (40:3–5). But that does not deny him the right to speak boldly from his pit of misery. Nor does God denounce him for his honesty. Job has been taken on a tour of the first days of creation and discovered the depths of God's wisdom (see comments on chaps. 38–39). Like the First Man, Job now appreciates the overwhelming complexity of it all. Now he is willing to remain silent.

Job had suffered unjustly and demanded redress. God responded with a show of wisdom and a challenge to demonstrate heroic glory and might. An instructive reversal of this pattern appears in the NT when James and John, the sons of thunder, request the privilege of being seated at either side of Jesus when he assumed his position of glory (Matt 20:20–23). They requested royal power. Jesus response is to offer them his baptism. They would experience the same suffering as Jesus and know the agony of unjust persecution. The response of the Lord to the demands of humans is often the reverse of our expectations, especially when we take on God.

If we explore this divine challenge by investigating the relationship of integrity and power we are forced to struggle with a problem faced by many individuals, groups and nations. Does power necessarily corrupt? Is there a power of a different order espoused by Job and Jesus? If we compare this passage with Luke 22:24–30 we can develop a sermon on the Power Alternatives:

(A) Power Without Integrity

    (1) Such is the way of despots, gangsters and many so-called benefactors (cf. Luke 22:25)

    (2) Such is Job's accusation against God (9:11–22; 12:13–22)

    (3) Are we immune from the desire for power at any cost? Do we manipulate people, even our family, to our own ends?

(B) Power With Integrity
  (1) Is it possible? This is apparently God's challenge to Job in 40:6–14. If Job can match God's might and demonstrate righteous power over the forces of evil, God will pay homage to Job as victor.
  (2) Job rejects God's challenge. Job's integrity alone is at stake!
  (3) No test of power will prove who is right. Even righteous might does not make right!
(C) Integrity as Power
  (1) Job is so unwavering in his integrity that God finally acknowledges Job to be "right" (42:7–8).
  (2) His oath of integrity has the power to move God; he even thunders his reply from a tempest.
  (3) But not everyone wins public approval for his or her integrity. Job, Jesus, Gandhi and Martin Luther King are exceptions, not the rule.
(D) Integrity Without Power
  (1) The challenge of Christ is to serve, not to pursue power (Luke 22:26–27). In his Kingdom roles are reversed.
  (2) He is the suffering servant, seeking our integrity, not his own. We in turn are servants who find integrity in him.
  (3) To serve is to impart life and integrity; "power" is a special gift from Christ (see Luke 22:28–30).

And Dust to Dust (42:1–6)

Job is all but struck dumb. The whirlwind of Yahweh was rather overwhelming. Job had long since acknowledged God's almighty power. In fact, that was one of his problems (see comments on 9:1–24). He had no desire to usurp God's role and play superman or supergod. Now that God's creation power is arrayed before Job, he experiences that reality anew. Job is impressed. The Almighty is mighty; when he plots something it happens, whether for good or ill (v. 2).

Two of God's replies keep ringing in Job's ears: "Who on earth is this man who hides God's counsel" (v. 3) and "I will ask the questions, you will answer" (v. 4). The questions God poses have no ready answers. They raise more questions, cryptic questions about the mysteries of the universe. Job has waded in too deep for comfort; he has attempted to handle cosmic riddles "too wonderful" for words (v. 3). He admits the mystery is beyond him.

What else could Job say? Whether grudgingly or willingly he capitulates and returns to the dust. There comes a point where humans like Job may return to the dust, not by necessity but by choice. From that idea a sermon can grow: "One With The Dust!" In his patient period Job had cried, "Naked I came from my mother's womb and naked I shall return there." Earth was a welcome mother to whom he would return; the grave would be his eventual home. Now something so profound, so overwhelming, has happened that renders his past understanding of God somewhat trifling. He now "sees God," albeit through the onslaught of a whirlwind. "Seeing God" was to be the result of the redeemer's efforts on Job's behalf. He was to see Job upon the dust and there be vindicated (see comments on 19:25–27). When he finally sees God, however, his response is one of self-negation. He has nowhere to go but to the dust. He has committed no crime, yet he can find no justice. He has challenged God's ways yet been flabbergasted by God's might as Creator and Ruler of the world. But the dust he knows. It spells humanness, the very stuff of life. To be dust in the hands of this Creator could mean nothing or it could mean everything. With that ambiguous confession Job is silent. Could any who lived his agony have discovered more?

When Job says "I repent" he is not expressing sorrow over sin or remorse over guilt. He does not confess, "I have been self-righteous," though we might have expected him to do so if we thought as Eliphaz does. He does not even admit that his assertion about unjust treatment at the hands of God was false. His "repentance" is a change of attitude, an acknowledgement that there are levels of divine mystery and might which he cannot grasp. What he knows is the world of dust and ashes. There he can find life as a human not as a superhuman.

The final words of another man reduced to the dust were, "Father, into thy hands I commit my spirit." From the dust, his spirit rose forth a new creation. Dust is the good stuff of creation. The Father gives life to the dust and the wisdom to ask why. That is the riddle of Job.

To know that we are dust, however, is to know that we are mortal. We may affirm or deny that reality in the way we struggle with our God. "Dust To Dust" is indeed an appropriate sermon theme. I experienced mortality in all its harshness at the funeral of a friend. He was the only true saint I knew personally, a man cut down in the prime of his wisdom. A bitter snow pelted the mourners at the graveside. Death seemed to penetrate my body and I felt strangely one with the rigid corpse of a beloved friend. I felt my death, my dust, my dying. So I commend this topic as powerful: "Dust to Dust."

(A) Denying Our Dust

    (1) By the camouflage of death at funerals, the hiding of age in corners, and the removal of the dying to hospitals.

    (2) By the cosmetics of a youth culture, the false images of eternal beauty, the paths to immortality.

    (3) By the daily competition to be the greatest, the smartest, the hero—and hereby ignoring our clay feet.

    (4) By refusing to discuss our mortality, our dying, our frailty, our facades, and our humanness.

    (5) By refusing to face our origin as clay, humans born of humans, not gods.

(B) Affirming Our Dust

    (1) In our sickness—Job calls his disease a clothing of worms and dust (RSV "dirt," 7:5); they are the marks of mortality coming out on him.

    (2) In our moments of dread—when we sense our end, the sick feeling within when we anticipate as real the day we will be but a corpse (see Job 14).

    (3) In our struggle with God—when we refuse to deny our humanity before God; in Job's case it meant asserting his integrity.

    (4) In our repentance—turning from self-sufficiency as mortals, to him who creates life out of dust (Eph 5:1, 14; Col 2:12; 3:10) through Christ.

    (5) In our grave—knowing our oneness with the saints in the dust—Abraham, Job, Jesus; and asserting that sleepers of the dust will arise (1 Cor 15:36–37; Isa 26:19).

How to Handle Prosperity (42:7–17)

What an ending! Prosperity of this order is enough to turn the head of a hero, to say nothing of a victim like Job. The reader, of course, has travelled through forty chapters of vehement poetic discourse. We know the violent Job of the great debate. The ending, however, is a happy conclusion to the folk story of Job, the pious patriarch (chaps. 1–2). The happy ending (42:10b–16) is carefully linked with the suffering Job of the poem by an important transition unit (vv. 7–10a). This unit suggests a way of handling reconciliation and achieving restoration.

God again breaks his silence and informs the three friends that he is not really angry at Job at all. Job was honest. His blunt accusations were closer to what was "right" than all their wise theology (v. 7). If Job is humbled in the poem, the friends are humiliated in the story. Job, who had longed for a redeemer to espouse his cause before God, now finds himself in the position of mediator on behalf of his friends. He had demanded justice and found a measure of wisdom. They had claimed wisdom and now find an agent of mercy. Reconciliation and renewal of the community are achieved through Job's priestly role as intercessor.

In the mediator Jesus Christ, justice, wisdom and mercy are all offered through vicarious suffering more profound than that of Job. Job is a prototype, a summons to acknowledge the eternal worth of the innocent victim. In Jesus Christ that worth is given divine validation and made available for all to appropriate. Those who suffer unjustly have Job as a friend and Jesus Christ as a redeemer. Prosperity is an optional plus.

Conclusion

Walking through the personal world of a suffering individual is a painful experience both for the sufferer and the friend. Walking through the life of Job is like travelling through a series of strange worlds, each fraught with dangers and trials. The interpretation of what we discover in the ancient folktale, the harsh rhetoric of Job, the traditional speeches of his wise friends, or the overwhelming challenge of his God, requires an appreciation of the poetic language, bold theology, and wisdom traditions of the book of Job. At the appropriate points these concerns have been tackled in this text.

Christian preaching from Job, however, demands a further set of skills and sensitivities. Job must be related to the NT where the search of Job is continued along new lines of hope and meaning. The advent of Christ adds new dimensions to the quest of Job.

Job is not only theology—it is also life! The book reflects the mental anguish of a wisdom writer who knew the power and meaning of suffering. The pain of Job comes through the poem of this writer. The trauma of Job's antagonism toward his God is an existential reality with which we can identify. The despair of a man without friends on earth or a merciful advocate in heaven touches us today—in spite of our affluence. Job loses his affluence and finds life; he loses his piety and finds God. These and similar themes for preaching are suggested in our commentary.

Whether or not we follow the Lenten cycle of sermons from Job proposed in the introduction, a rich set of lively issues about faith in the context of the real world emerge through the pages of Job. If we dare to preach in terms consistent with the realism and passion expressed by Job, we will reach a depth of spiritual concern in our people. We will speak to the pain, the emotions, and the fears of their faith. We may even be moved to offer litanies of anger or liturgies of conflict that enable spiritual catharsis for worshippers today in ways similar to those experienced by Job.

The preacher has a mandate from the Book of Job to enable human conflict with God to be expressed and handled, at least through the sermon. God is experienced anew in the agonizing struggles of those who dare to challenge the suffering and despair of life and who confront God with the terrors of his own world. Preaching from Job involves living with a complex text and struggling with a complex God. But then, I never promised you a rose garden!